LAKE TAMARISK

IMAGES
of America

BLYTHE AND THE
PALO VERDE VALLEY

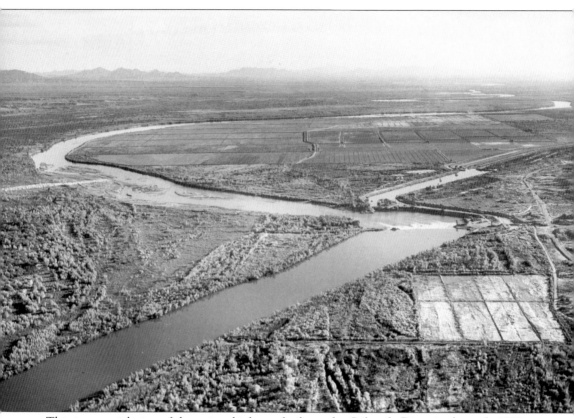

This is an aerial view of the weir, which was built on the Colorado River in the early 1900s at the north end of the Palo Verde Valley to facilitate the irrigation of the valley. It was replaced by a dam in the 1950s.

IMAGES
of America

BLYTHE AND THE PALO VERDE VALLEY

Palo Verde Historical Museum and Society

ARCADIA
PUBLISHING

Published by Arcadia Publishing
Charleston SC, Chicago IL, Portsmouth NH, San Francisco CA

Printed in the United States of America

Library of Congress Catalog Card Number: 2005931988

For all general information contact Arcadia Publishing at:
Telephone 843-853-2070
Fax 843-853-0044
E-mail sales@arcadiapublishing.com
For customer service and orders:
Toll-Free 1-888-313-2665

Visit us on the Internet at www.arcadiapublishing.com

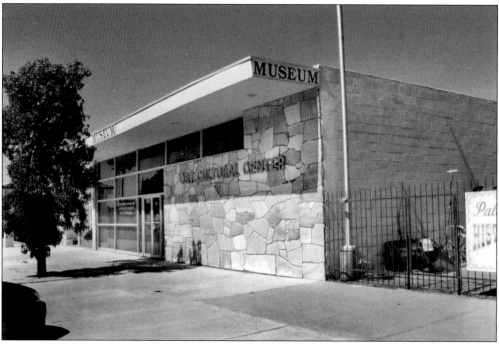

Pictured is the current home of the Palo Verde Historical Museum and Society located at 150 North Broadway in Blythe.

CONTENTS

ACKNOWLEDGMENTS

This book was compiled by Sylvia Summers and Marilee Harkinson, members of the Palo Verde Historical Museum and Society's current board of directors.

This book would not have been possible without the dedication and hard work of three of the founding members of the museum: Nancy Graham, Erin Port, and Margaret Port. Thanks to their leadership and dedication, the museum has been able to preserve the history of Blythe and the Palo Verde Valley.

We encourage all of you to visit the museum at the Port Cultural Center, 150 North Broadway in Blythe, California.

INTRODUCTION

In 1877, O. P. Callaway made a leisurely trip up the Colorado River from Yuma to explore the gold-mining town of La Paz, Arizona. On a spot opposite the declining town of Ehrenberg, in the tree enshrouded lowlands, Callaway, an engineer, saw the possibilities of a man-made paradise using water from the Colorado River.

With no money of his own, Callaway returned to San Francisco and contacted Thomas H. Blythe. Blythe, born Thomas Williams in Mold, Wales, in 1822, left England in 1849, changed his name to Blythe, landed in San Francisco, and made a fortune in real estate and mining.

Under the provisions approved by an act of Congress on September 11, 1850, states were able to reclaim swampland and overflow lands within their limits. Blythe filed on some 44,000 acres and then claimed 95,000 inches of water from the Colorado River that would come through a ditch on Olive Slough. This ditch was to be cut 124 feet wide and 4 feet deep. He also claimed 95,000 inches of water to be taken out at Black Point. The ditches were to be brought together and carried in a main canal to be known as the Desert Land Canal.

Blythe only visited the valley twice but poured $82,000 into the project and called it Blythe City. At the time, his "city" consisted of a tule hut or two, a store surrounded by a mesquite wood and rawhide corral, and a few acres of cleared land. Blythe then hired George S. Irish as his representative and general manager. On arriving in the valley, Irish and Callaway, with American Indian labor, started building a rock headgate in the riverbank to irrigate the entire valley.

By the end of 1878, Callaway had completed a temporary canal and constructed a 40-acre experimental farm. They planted corn, beans, alfalfa, melons, sugar cane, and cotton. By the following May, it was known as the Colorado Colony, with land offered for sale at $8 per acre, including water rights. Callaway was killed during a confrontation with American Indians shortly thereafter. He was buried near the main canal under a small mesquite tree.

On the evening of April 4, 1883, Thomas Blythe was stricken with a heart attack and died. Work on the Palo Verde Project stopped abruptly. The estate of Thomas Blythe was thrown into litigation, which was not settled until 1904, when his daughter Florence was declared the heir. In late 1904, the Mutual Water Company was formed and purchased the Blythe property from Florence. Work slowly resumed. Early pioneers included Frank Murphy, Floyd Brown, Mr. Donlon, the Hobson brothers, and Edwin Williams.

The City of Blythe was incorporated in 1916, with a population of 600. The original city was 832 acres and had a $4,000 yearly budget.

In 1923, the Palo Verde Irrigation District was established to assume the duties previously performed by the Mutual Water Company, the Palo Verde Joint Levee District, and the Palo Verde Drainage District. The new district had 79,056 acres of land within its boundaries, with 36,135 in cultivation. The Palo Verde Valley continues to develop and evolve, its very existence made possible by the waters of the Colorado River.

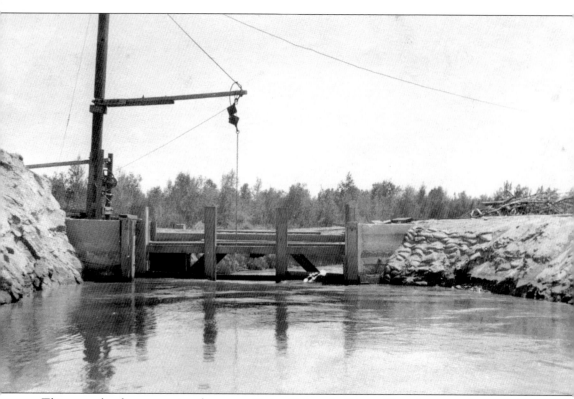

This was the first water-intake gate off the Colorado River. The photograph was taken before 1910.

One

THE EARLY YEARS
PRIOR TO 1910

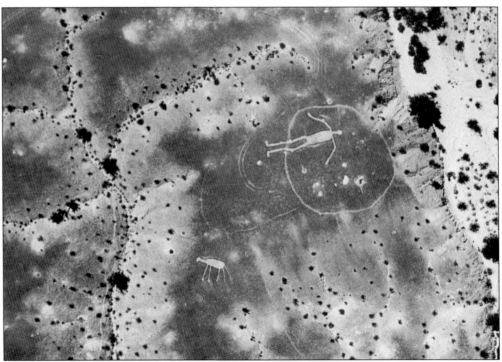

These American Indian desert drawings, estimated between 450 and 2,000 years old, are located just north of the Palo Verde Valley. According to Mohave and Queshan tribes of the lower Colorado River, the human figure represents Mastamho, the creator of earth and all life. The animal figure represents Hatakulya, one of two mountain lions/people who helped in the creation. There are many intaglios located in the desert that surrounds the valley. Most are best viewed from the air.

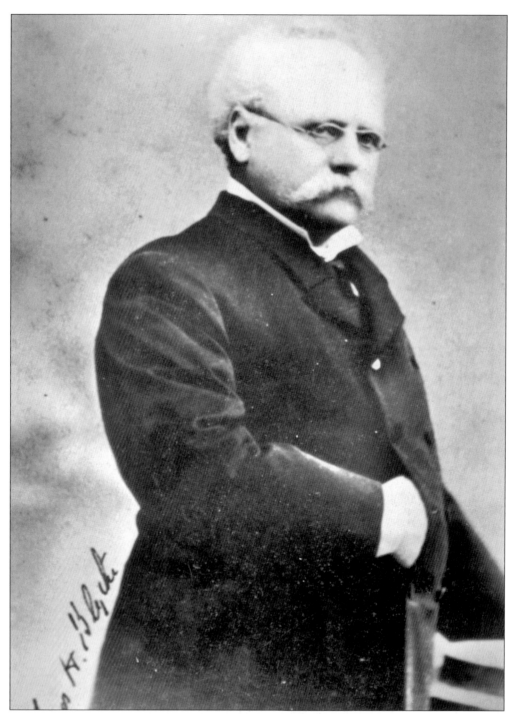

Although he only visited the Palo Verde Valley twice, Thomas H. Blythe, shown in this portrait, applied for and received the water rights for Colorado River water and financed the construction of the original irrigation system. Blythe passed away in 1883, which halted construction on the irrigation system. When his estate was settled in 1904, construction resumed.

10

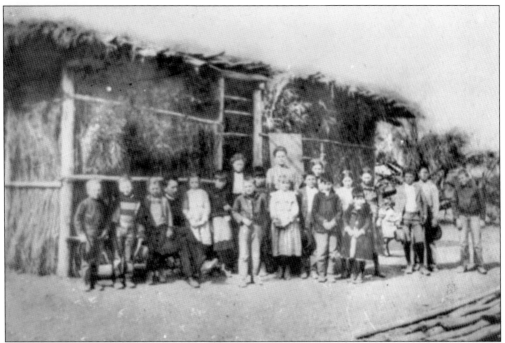

In 1902, the first school in the Palo Verde Valley, Arrowweed School, was established. Located approximately 100 yards east of the Palo Verde Lagoon, it was constructed of cottonwood poles and arrowweed. The first teacher was Ellen Decker, who later became Mrs. Lyman F. Norton. Her memoirs were published by the Palo Verde Historical Museum and Society in a book titled *Memoirs of a School Ma'am*.

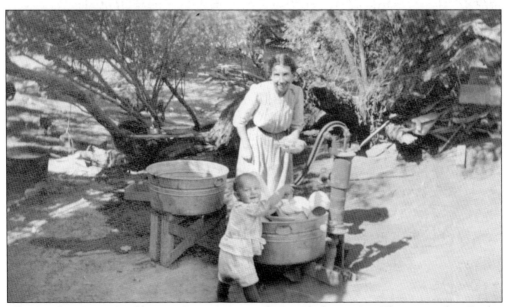

Ellen Decker Norton and her son Bert are pictured on wash day *c.* 1911. They are at their Ripley ranch, where they lived until 1917. Ellen helped organize the First Baptist Church and was the first president of the Blythe Women's Improvement Club.

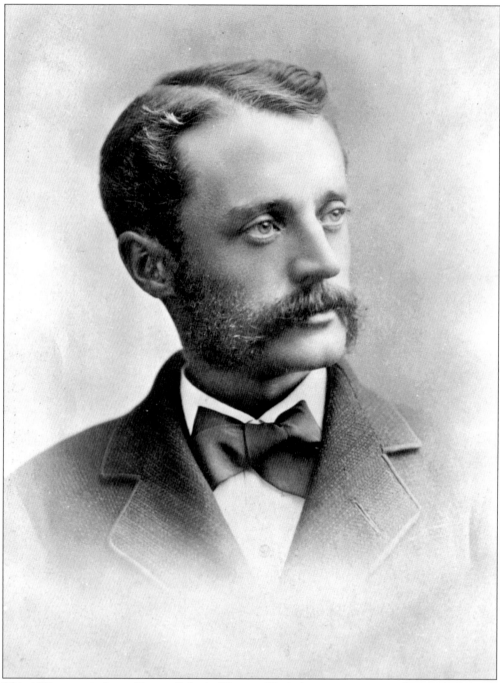

This 1881 portrait shows George S. Irish, Thomas Blythe's representative and general manager in the valley prior to Blythe's death in 1883. After Blythe's death, Irish left the valley and settled in San Diego.

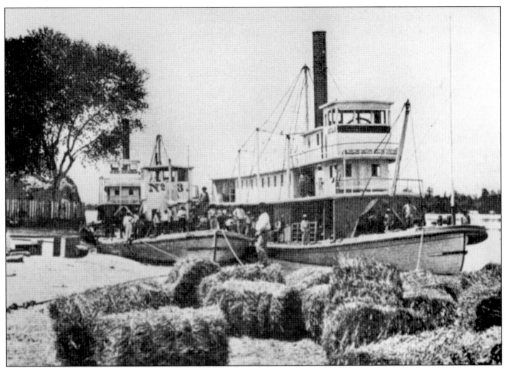

The steamboats pictured here, *Gila* and *Cocopah*, traveled up the Colorado River from Yuma, Arizona, and went as far north as Needles, California. They stopped at Ehrenberg, Arizona, which is directly across the Colorado River from the Palo Verde Valley.

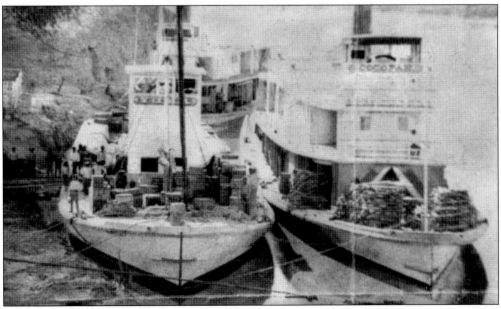

The steamboats *Cocopah*, *Yuma*, and *Queshan* are shown at dock in this 1875 photograph. The steamboats ran until 1909, when the Laguna Dam was built north of Yuma, Arizona, and stopped all river traffic.

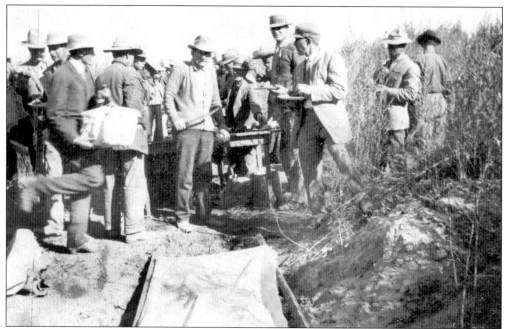

In 1907, a barbecue was held on the Blythe ranch, the headquarters for George Irish and O. P. Callaway during construction of the irrigation system.

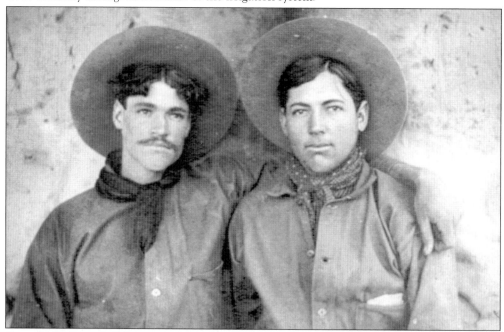

Pictured here are Ralph and Tony Seeley in 1909. At the time, the brothers were working as brush hands. In 1899, they came to the Cibola Valley, located south of Blythe across the Colorado River in Arizona, with their father. Ralph Seeley left the valley in 1912 and never returned. Tony Seeley later purchased land and became a farmer, but he never lost his love of being a cowboy. Tony's son Raymond grew up in the valley, farmed here, and raised racehorses. Raymond Seeley was later elected to the California State Senate.

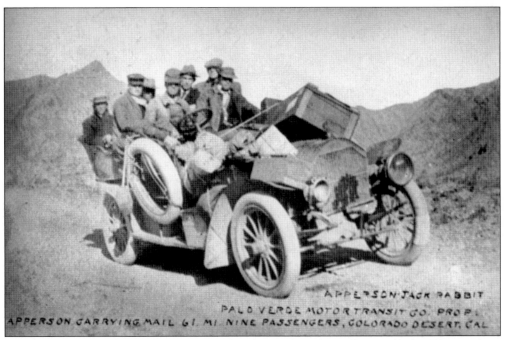

The Apperson Jackrabbit Stage carried mail and passengers from Yuma to Blythe. The trip from Glamis to the Blythe ranch house, a 70-mile journey, took two days. This photograph was taken in 1908. It looks like it was a rough way to travel.

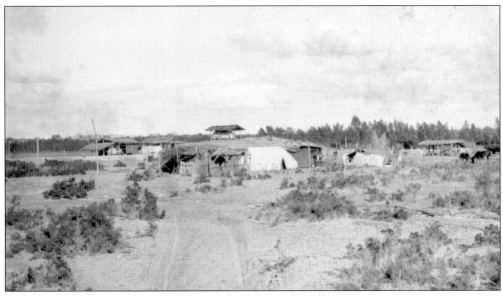

This is an early homestead somewhere in the Palo Verde Valley.

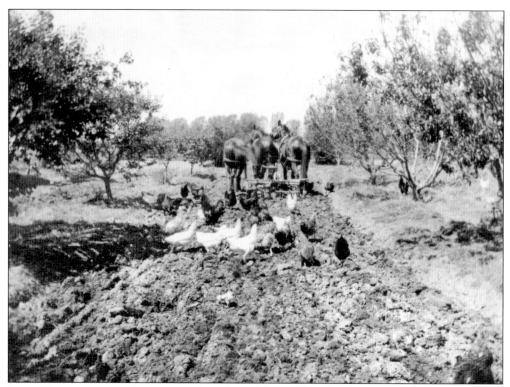

James Davenport, an early pioneer, plows the field to ready it for planting sweet potatoes.

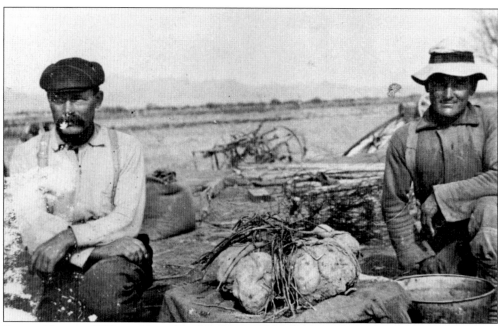

Pictured here in 1908 are Al and Basil DeMeyer. Note the sweet potatoes on the table between the two men.

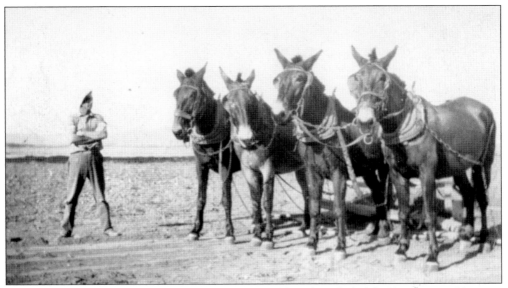

Jack Marlowe came to the valley in 1904 and farmed here his whole life. He is pictured here on his homestead in 1923. In his younger days, he fought in Mexico against Pancho Villa. He served on the Palo Verde Irrigation Board of Directors for seven years and was active in the Blythe Lions Club and the chamber of commerce. The horses were named Dick, Buck, Bearcat, and Joe.

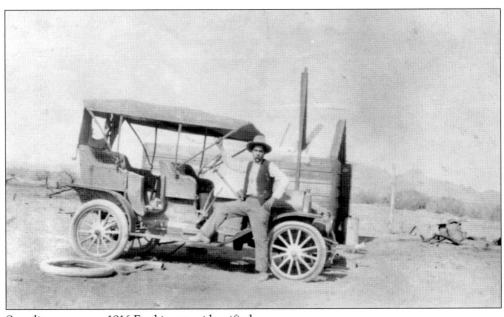

Standing next to a 1916 Ford is an unidentified man.

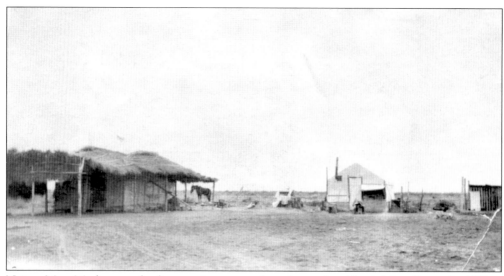

Neipps Meat Market was the first one in town and was located on North Main Street. In 1911, it advertised fresh beef for sale at 10¢ per pound. In 1919, Herman Neipp built a reinforced concrete structure to house the market.

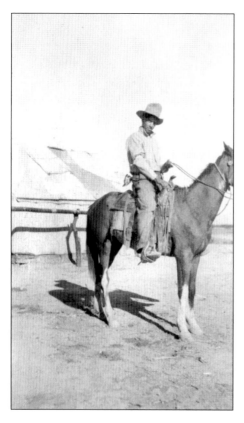

Around 1910, Tom Wells poses on his horse. Tom came to the valley in 1903 with his family, who traveled by wagon train from Kansas. He was the world-champion relay rider seven times and participated in rodeos around the entire country. He also worked as a guide for mule trains at the Grand Canyon. He later owned and operated the Tom Wells Bar in Ehrenberg, Arizona, until his death.

Two

FOUNDATIONS
1910–1929

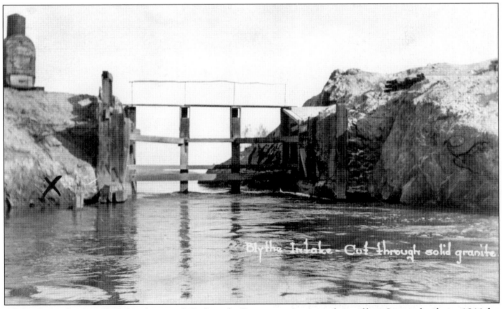

The original water intake diverted Colorado River water into the valley. It was built in 1911 by Palo Verde Mutual Water Company. This intake was cut through solid granite.

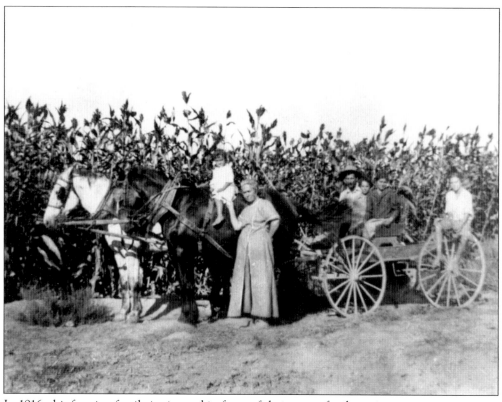

In 1916, this farming family is pictured in front of their crop of milo maize.

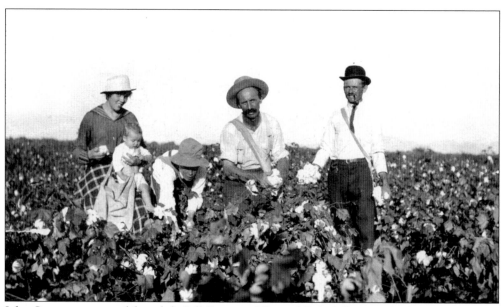

John Stevenson, second from left, Bill Root, middle, and Bob Gilliam, right, harvest cotton in this 1916 photograph. The Cotton Growers Association formed in 1911, and a steam-powered cotton gin was built the same year, allowing for a more efficient processing operation.

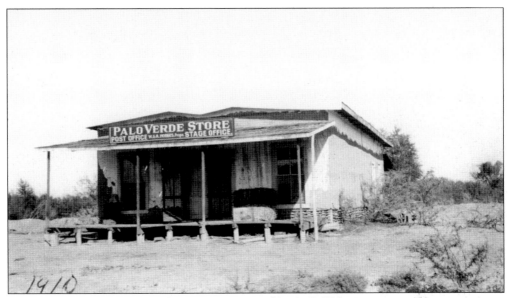

The Palo Verde Store, pictured in 1910, was owned by A. P. Wiley.

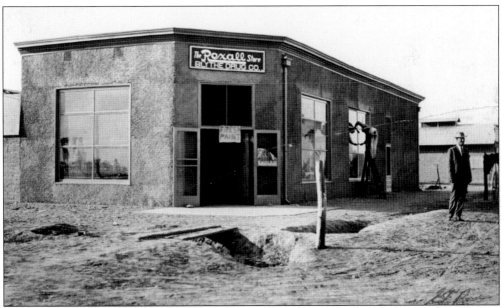

The original Blythe Drug Store building, pictured around 1915, was located on the corner of Hobsonway and Main Street. Standing in front of the building is Charles Utting, and the man on the ladder is Lon Rudd.

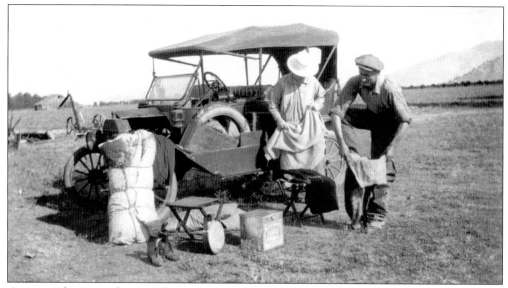

A man and woman change a flat tire.

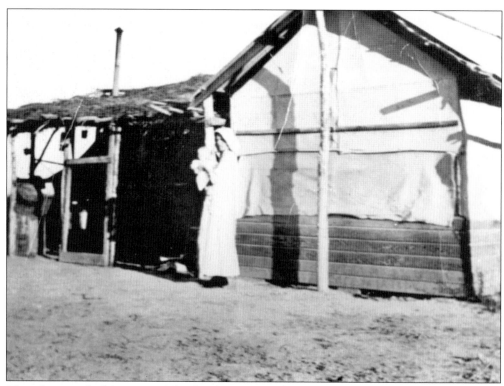

This photograph shows one of the first homes, representative of the living conditions for the period prior to 1915.

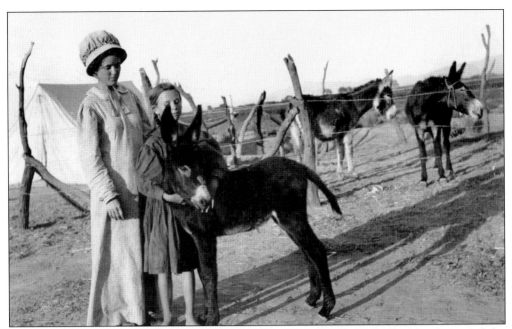

This was the Springer ranch in 1910. Pictured are Ione and Allene Buck with one of the ranch's donkeys.

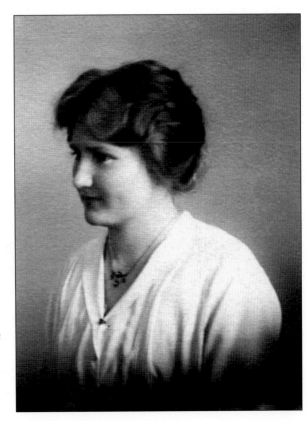

This 1917 portrait shows Leora M. Culpepper. She was the first graduate from Palo Verde High School and taught in the Palo Verde Valley School District for many years. She later married Val Buck, a rancher in the valley.

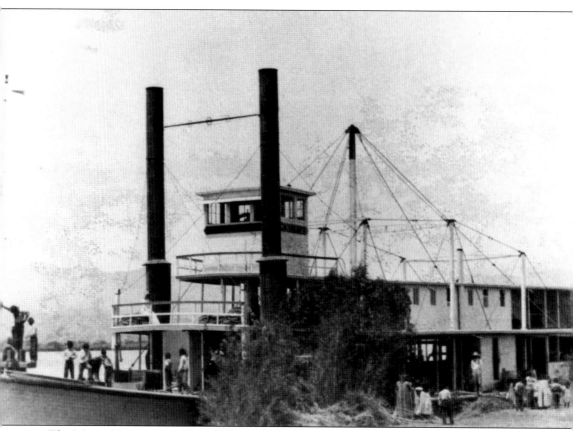

The *Mojave II* was a steamboat that traveled between Yuma and Ehrenberg, Arizona.

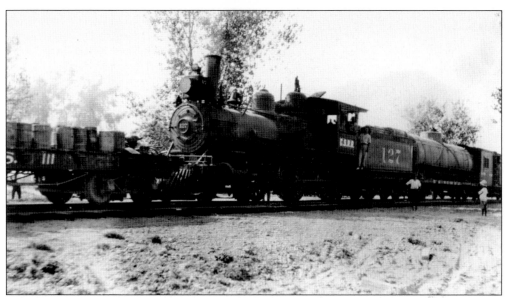

On August 8, 1916, the first train, operated by the Southern California Railroad, arrived in Blythe. The first shipment out of the valley was a load of hogs, owned by Rudolph Ehlers, destined for a Los Angeles market. Mrs. J. M. Neeland purchased the first ticket from Blythe to Los Angeles for $13.20. With the arrival of the railroad, mail delivery was possible six days a week.

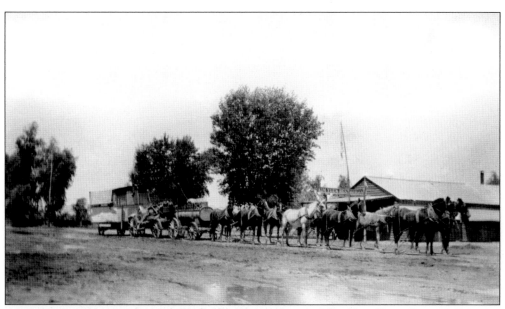

A grading outfit coming into Blythe looks northwest. The Kim Yuen Restaurant is in the background.

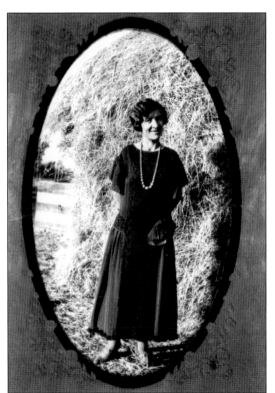

Mrs. Cooper was a teacher at Arrowhead School, which opened in 1919 and closed in 1942. It was located on the corner of Arrowhead and Riverside Drives.

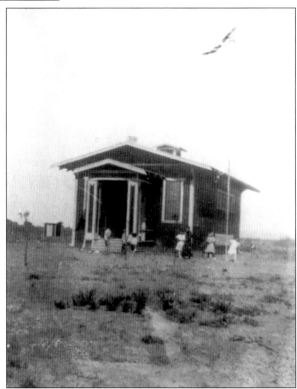

Rocky Comfort School is pictured here in 1917. Note the outhouse behind the school.

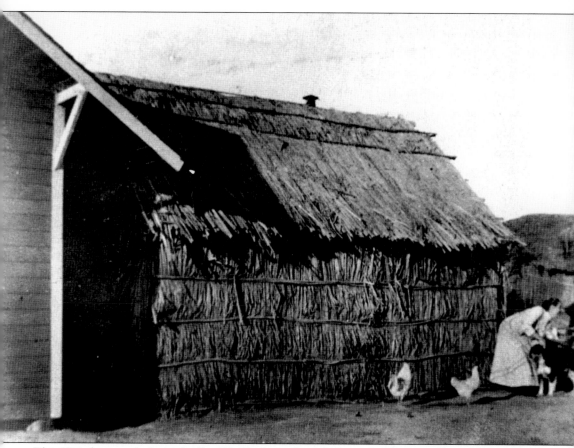

This 1914 photograph shows the Basil DeMeyer ranch, with Carrie DeMeyer standing next to a tule room addition. Basil DeMeyer came to America from Belgium in 1897 and settled in Waukegan, Illinois. There he helped his mother on the farm and worked in a manufacturing plant making things such as baling wire. Tired of the cold winters and convinced by his brother Alidore, who had been West, he decided to look for warmer climes. Alidore had told him of farm land for sale in the Palo Verde Valley for $40 per acre. In 1907, Basil, brother Alidore, and cousin Camiel Dekens took the train to Glamis, California. There they caught a $20 wagon ride to Blythe, where DeMeyer worked as a teamster for Palo Verde Land and Water Company, saved his money, and bought some farm land on North Lovekin. In June 1920, he married Lillian Monnot, and they became the first couple to be married in St. Joan of Arc Catholic Church. They built a house in the Eastern style, with living quarters on top and livestock underneath. The family raised nine children—seven boys and two girls—and grew various crops, including melons and sweet potatoes, along with alfalfa and grain to feed dairy cows and beef stock. The pecan trees they planted along the canal bank are still producing there. DeMeyer's beef took top prices at the Los Angeles market. After his death, DeMeyer's farm was sold to Sax Eaton, a young farmer new to the valley. Sax built a stucco house surrounded by Basil's pomegranate, citrus, and pecan trees.

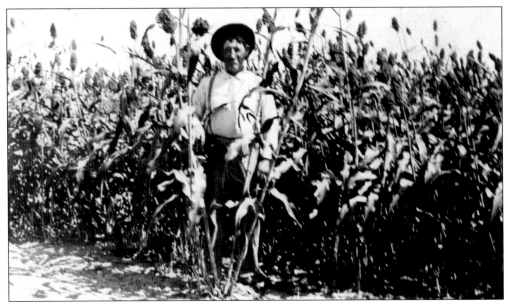

In 1914, Mr. Neipp stands in front of his milo maize. This photograph is representative of early farming operations in the valley.

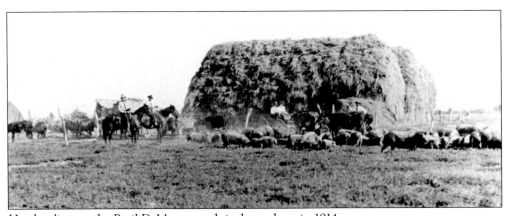

Hog herding on the Basil DeMeyer ranch is shown here in 1914.

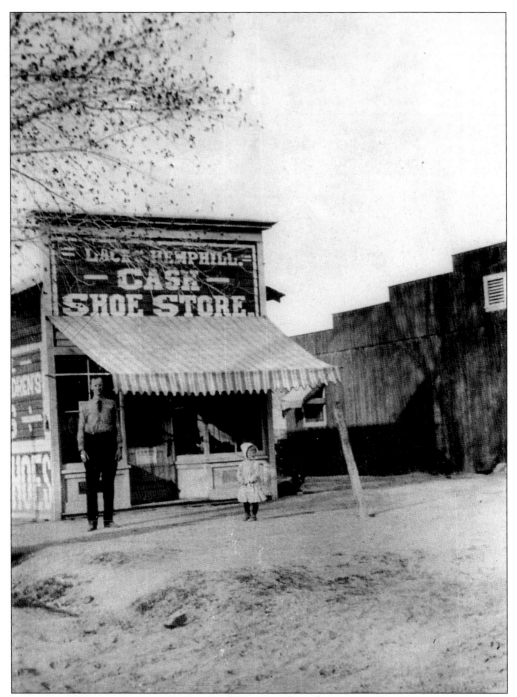

Lace Hemphill and his daughter Barbara pose in front of Hemphill's Shoe Store in 1916. Lace and his wife, Lois, came to the valley in 1910. Although he was a master plumber, he found little work and, in 1911, decided to open a shoe store. He later became the deputy county clerk and even issued marriage licenses in the early days. Lace's son Warren served many years as the manager of the chamber of commerce. The shoe store was continuously run as a family business until November 30, 2002.

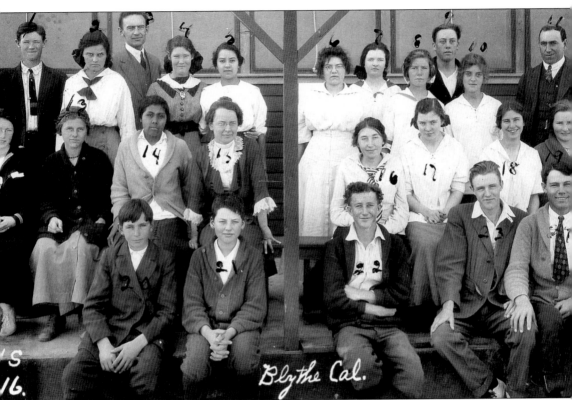

Students from the Palo Verde High School, pictured here in 1916, from left to right, are (first row) Willie Glace, Cyril Jurez, Dave Hill, Arno Sims, and Jessie Hill; (second row) Ruth Darling, Dorothy Wolford, Aurora Lugo, Mrs. Beck, Minnie White, Emma Rains, Alleen Buck, and Leora Culpepper; (third row) Bud Bates, Eva Mulkey, ? Newman, Irene Bates, Josephine Daniels, Phyllis Jaurez, Theresa Fawcett, Virgie Fitz, Paul Ochletree, Muriel Burgess, and ? Bentel. The high school district was formed in 1914, and Union High School was built the same year. It was located at the intersection of Hobsonway and Seventh Street.

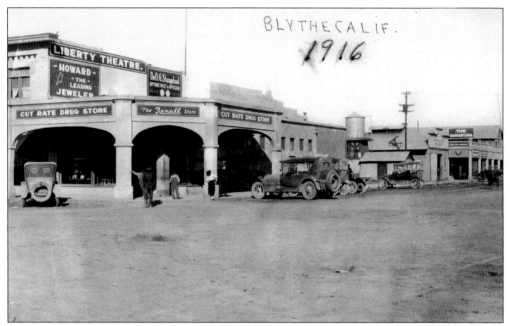

This 1916 street scene shows the corner of Hobsonway and Main Street, which included a theatre, an optometrist, and a drug store. Note the small water tower in the background.

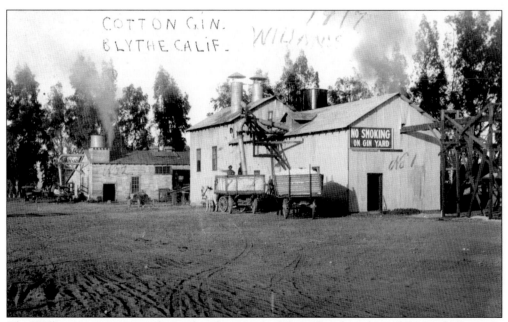

The William cotton gin was located at the corner of the railroad tracks and Riverside Drive. In 1917, it was shipped to the valley from Georgia. The R&R Mini Mart is now located there.

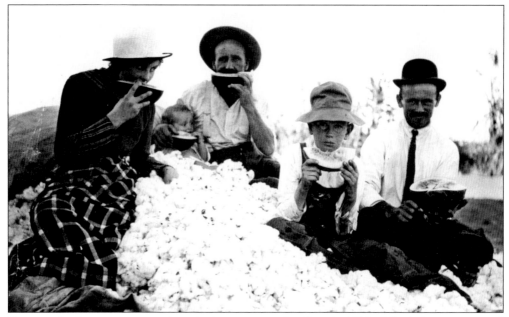

These early pioneers appear to be enjoying a watermelon feast in 1916 while sitting on a mound of cotton. The southern custom of planting watermelons between the rows of cotton was carried on in the valley. The melons ripened during cotton picking time and eating them as a pleasant break for the pickers.

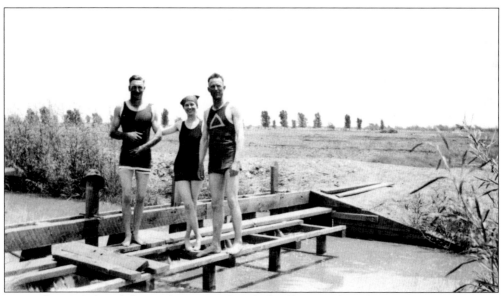

Pictured c. 1918, from left to right, are unidentified, Allene Buck, and George King. It was not unusual to see swimmers in the canals, as it was much safer than swimming in the river.

This was an early 1900s saloon located in Ehrenberg, Arizona.

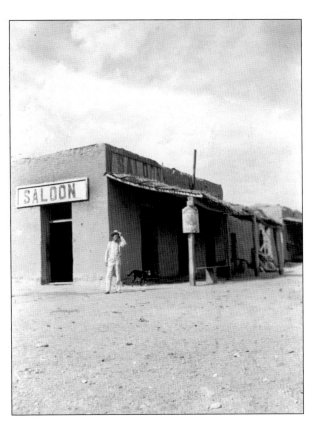

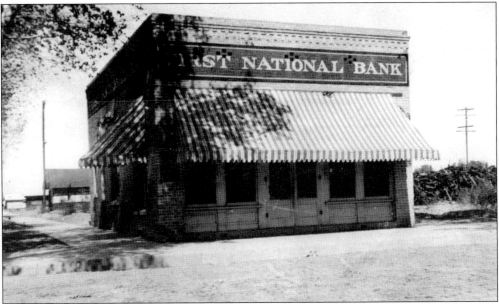

The First National Bank was located on the northeast corner of Hobsonway and Broadway. When this bank was robbed in December 1913, a cashier was killed and a total of $4,446 was taken. The burglars were later caught in El Centro, California. They were asleep, and the money was found under their bed. The First National Bank of Blythe is pictured here in 1916.

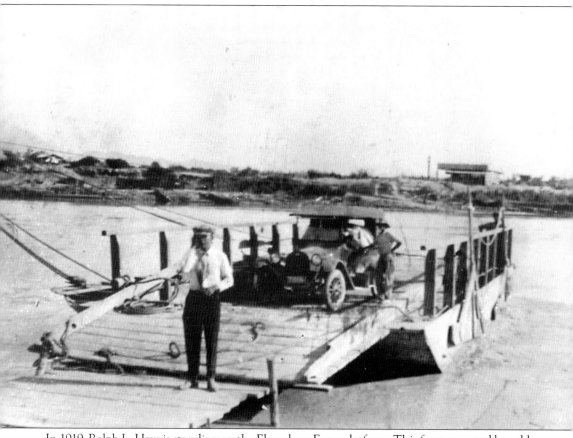

In 1919, Ralph L. Hays is standing on the Ehrenberg Ferry platform. This ferry operated by cables running across the river. Normally less than 40 vehicles per day used the ferry service.

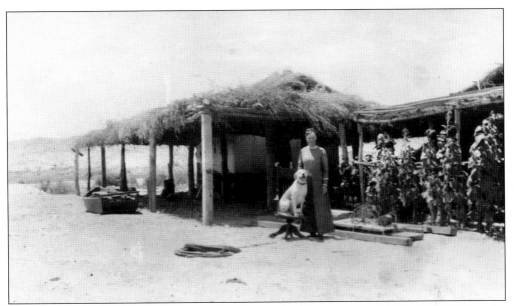

This was the north water intake caretaker's house, seen here between 1913 and 1915. Note the dog perched on the chair.

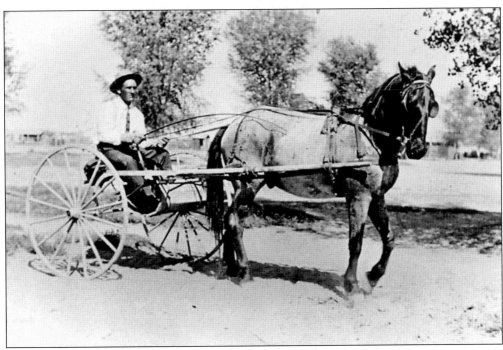

This 1914 portrait of Basil DeMeyer was taken on the DeMeyer ranch.

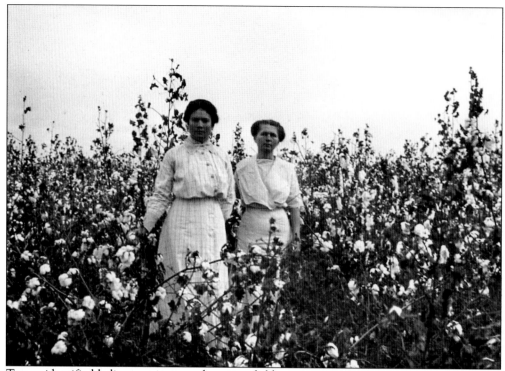

Two unidentified ladies pose in an early cotton field.

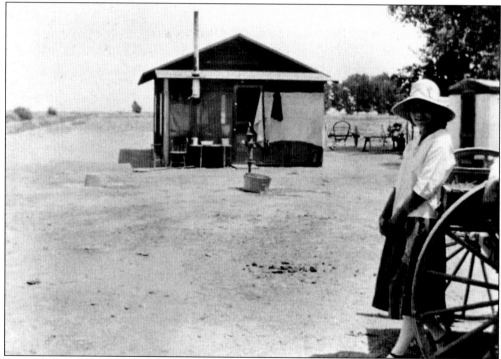

An early homestead, located at the corner of Rannels and Neighbors Boulevards, is seen here in 1919. Pictured is Gertrude Monnot. Her sister Lillian married Basil DeMeyer in 1920.

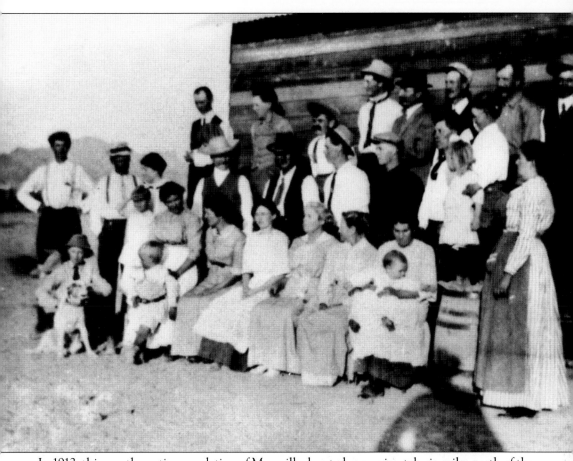

In 1912, this was the entire population of Mesaville, located approximately six miles north of the Palo Verde Valley. Established in 1909 by about 100 homesteaders, the plan was to grow citrus, and a deep well was dug for a water source. The well proved to be inadequate, and plans were made to drill another one, but a hard freeze occurred in 1912 and the citrus trees were lost. Discouraged, most of the residents moved away, but a store and post office remained open until 1916.

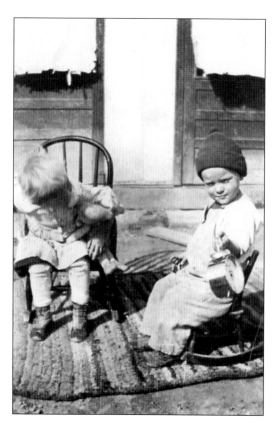

Eugenia and Lawrence Rains Jr. are pictured here in 1915. The Rains family lived on North Second Street in Blythe. Lawrence Rains Sr. came to the valley in 1910. He and his brother Jack owned the Ford car dealership. He was known as a master mechanic and was frequently called upon to repair machinery at the Palo Verde Creamery and the *Palo Verde Valley Times* newspaper.

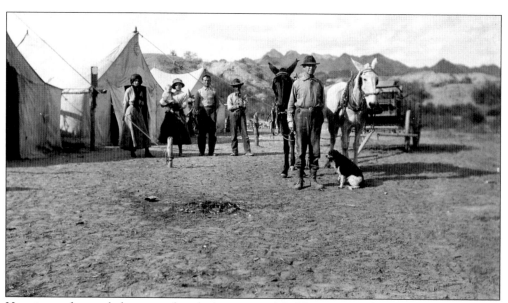

Here is another early homestead with three tents. Mr. Neipp is standing in front of his light spring wagon.

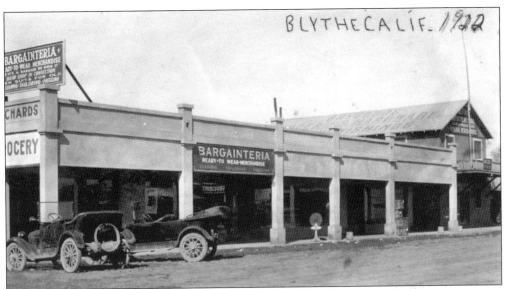

In 1922, clothes shopping in Blythe consisted of the Bargainteria, which sold ready-to-wear merchandise. It was owned by W. H. Minerman and Walter Walsh. Minerman was a leader in the fight to get good roads into the valley.

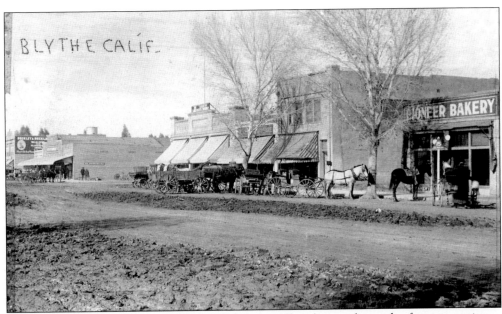

This late-1910 Blythe street scene shows a bakery as well as the popular mode of transportation— horse and buggy.

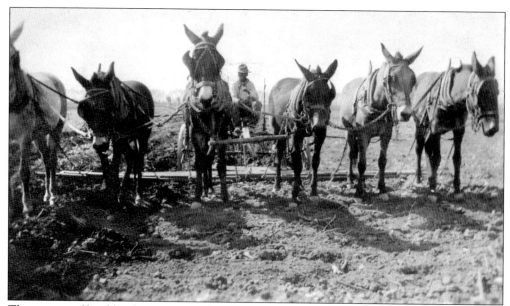

The process of land leveling uses a six-horse hitch, as seen in this 1920 photograph.

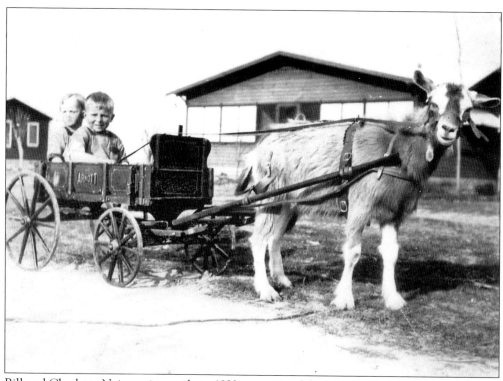

Bill and Charlotte Neipp enjoy a ride in 1922, courtesy of their goat.

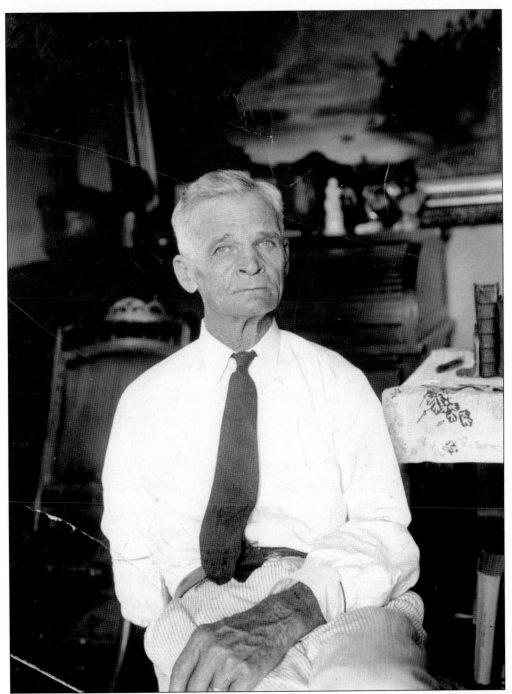

Ed Williams came to the valley in 1904, left, and returned in 1908. He was instrumental in laying out the levee and drainage system in the valley. In the early 1930s, he made three trips to Washington, D.C., to secure funding after the Palo Verde Irrigation District was forced to default on $4 million in bonds during the Great Depression. He was president of the chamber of commerce for 25 years. While he was on the water board, he and C. K. Clarke, an engineer, rebuilt the entire canal system.

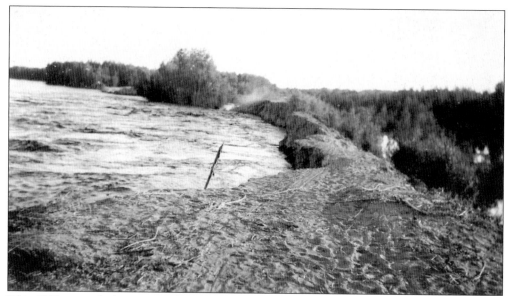

This 1922 view of a levee was taken two miles south of Hobsonway near Raab Bend. The river is just about to break through the levee. This flood was one of the worst ever, and two-thirds of the valley was underwater.

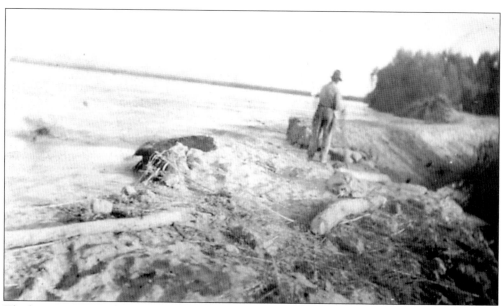

The levees were raised in 1913 after the valley experienced many levee breaks from 1909 to 1912. They weren't quite high enough, though, to prevent this break in 1922 at Hauser Bend.

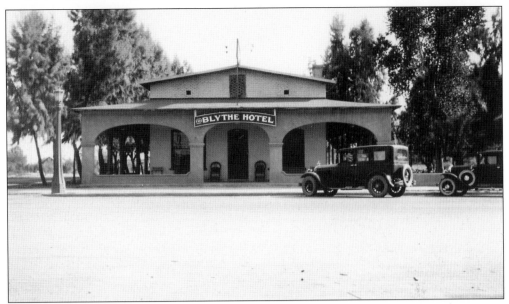

The Blythe Hotel, pictured here in the 1920s, was first operated by Peter D. McIntyre, who came to the valley in 1908. McIntyre farmed in his early years in the valley and is credited with organizing the first cotton association. He was also the first postmaster in Blythe and held that position for 40 years. Riverside County named a county park on the Colorado River after him.

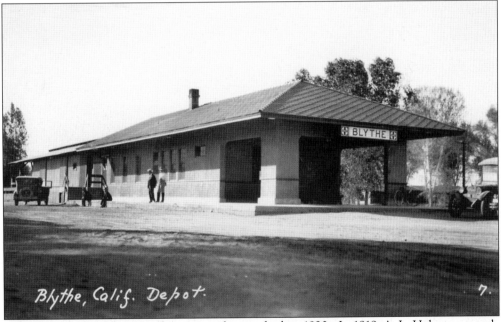

This photograph of the train depot was taken in the late 1920s. In 1919, A. L. Hobson, an early pioneer, drew the plans for this building. The depot, although not occupied, still stands just south of Hobsonway on the east side of railroad tracks. Hobsonway, the main street through Blythe, was named after A. L. Hobson.

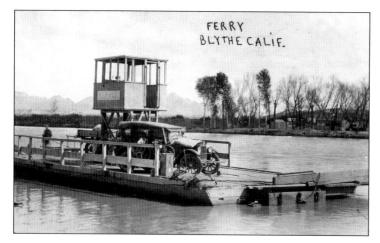

This 1922 view of the motorized ferry from Blythe to Ehrenberg, looks toward Arizona. It has been reported that the ferry netted $18,999 in a six-month period.

Construction work on the first bridge over the Colorado River began in the 1920s. Floyd Brown, a valley resident, was given the contract to build the bridge for $275,000. He bid too low, and another contractor finished the bridge in 1928.

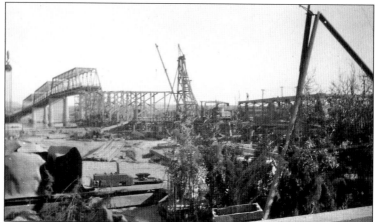

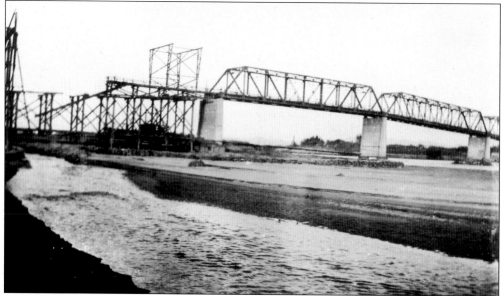

Work on the bridge is almost completed.

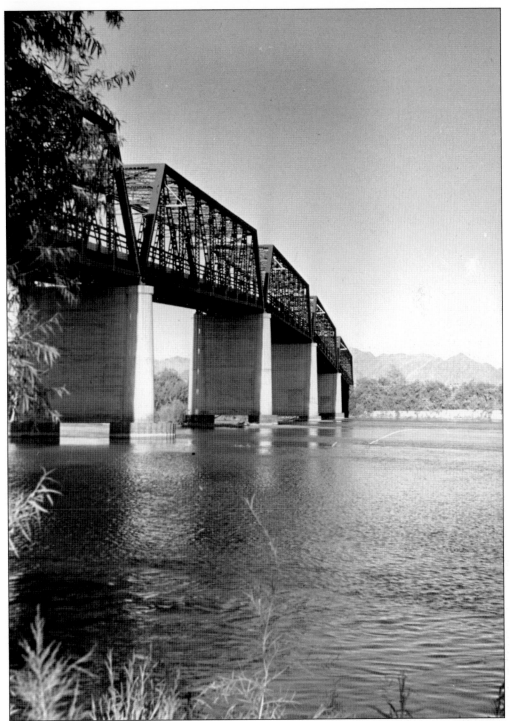

Looking east is the completed bridge project in 1929. Approximately 3,000 people attended the dedication ceremony. The ceremony was originally scheduled to include a program on the California side of the river, but the governor of Arizona, George Hunt, reportedly refused to go any further than the middle of the bridge.

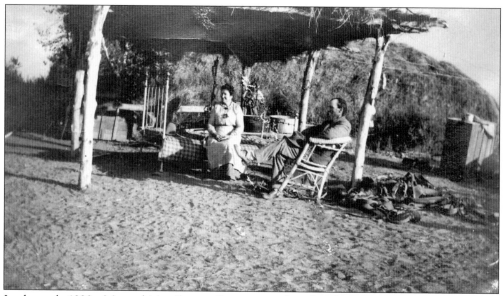

In the early 1920s, Mr. and Mrs. Eugene Rains sit in their first home on Rannels Boulevard. It was a trendsetter for open living spaces. Note the bed under the canopy.

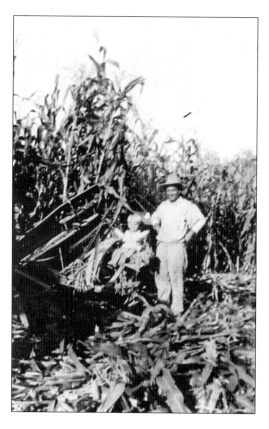

Basil DeMeyer and his son Vincent are harvesting corn in 1922. DeMeyer installed the first silos in the valley and raised purebred Herford cattle.

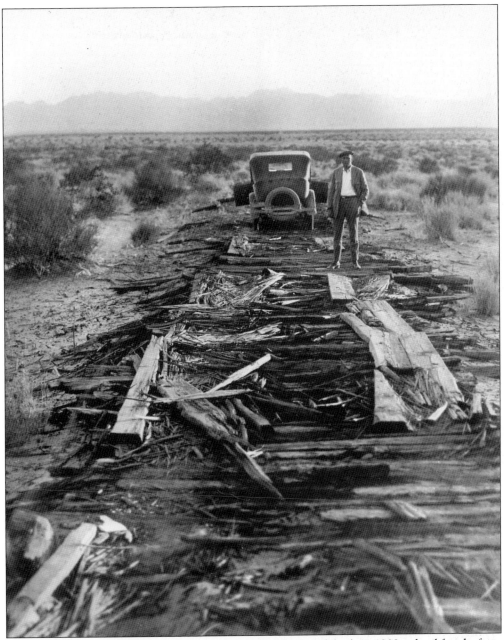

This was the original plank road to Rice, California. The road, built in 1909 to haul freight from Blythe to Rice, was located approximately 50 miles north of Blythe.

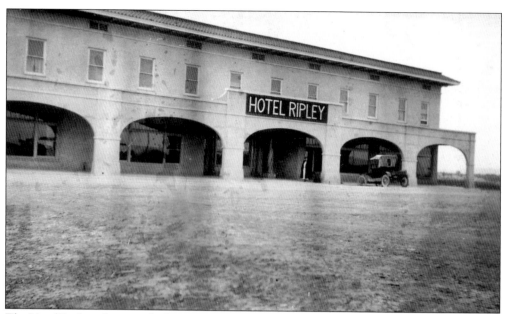

The Hotel Ripley, photographed in 1922 just after construction was completed, provided the most luxurious accommodations in the valley. It had 30 rooms and a dining area. The town of Ripley was named after E. P. Ripley from Chicago. He was the president of the Santa Fe Railroad and made an extensive tour of the valley in 1917.

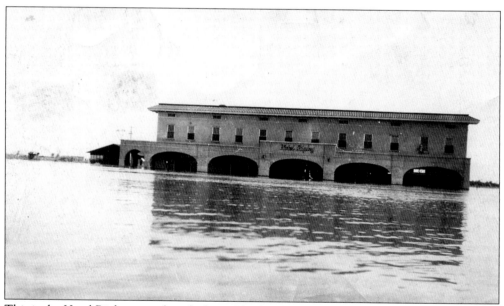

This is the Hotel Ripley several weeks later. The hotel was completely flooded by the Colorado River just weeks after it opened. Guests had to be rescued from the second story by rowboat. The hotel never reopened, but was used as a school temporarily.

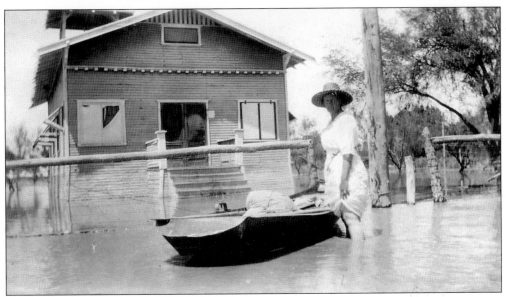

The Ripley School also flooded in 1922. It is estimated that 35,000 acres of farmland were covered with water. The City of Blythe escaped any damage, but Ripley and other low-lying areas were hard-hit.

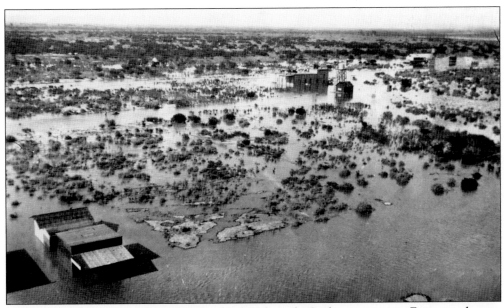

This is a panoramic view of the 1922 flood, taken from the Ripley water tower. Extensive damage resulted in the lower end of the valley.

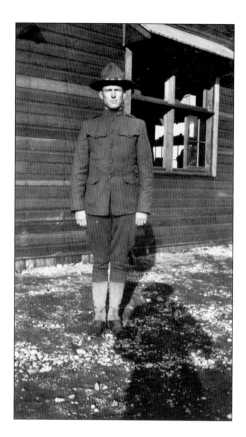

Mr. Val Buck, seen here in 1918 at Fort Lewis, was an early pioneer who served in the United States Army.

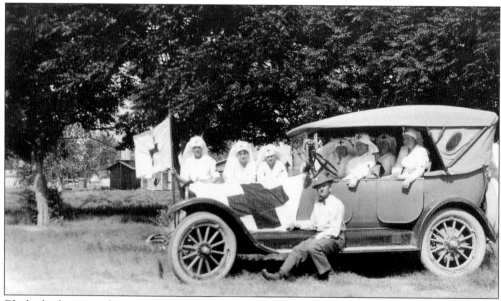

Blythe had many volunteers who participated in Red Cross activities during World War I.

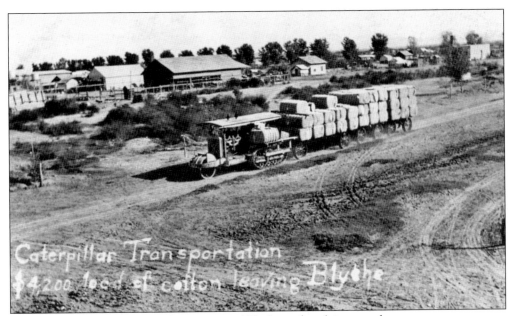

This Caterpillar tractor hauled cotton out of Blythe and took it to market.

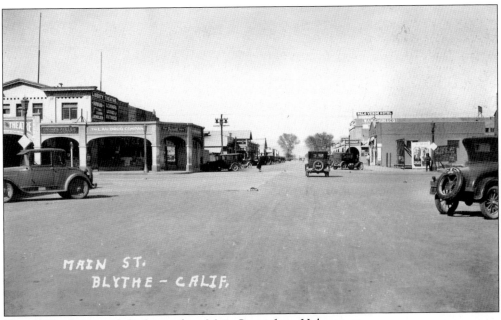

This 1920s photograph looks north to Main Street from Hobsonway.

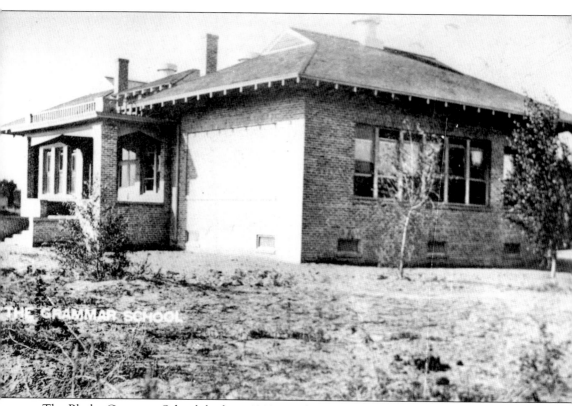

THE GRAMMAR SCHOOL

The Blythe Grammar School, built in 1909, was located on the corners of Murphy and First Streets. In later years, it was called the Margaret White School to honor Margaret White, the school's principal from 1924 to 1959. This building was torn down in the late 1950s.

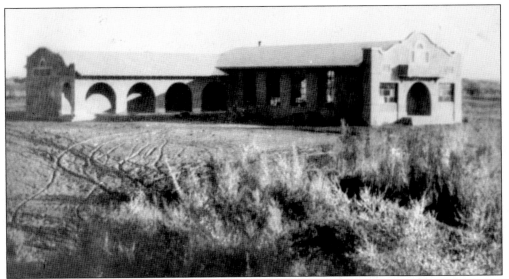

Appleby School was located on Bernard Street between Second and Third Streets, the site of the Methodist church.

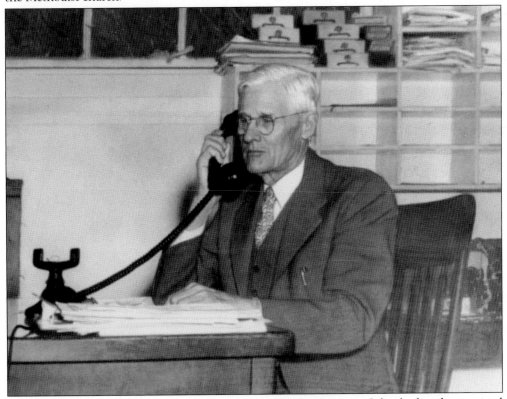

Felix J. Appleby came to Blythe in 1929 as principal of Blythe Grammar School, where he remained for 29 years. During his stay, the school was renamed Appleby Grammar School. A kind, gentle man, he was known to be firm when firmness was called for. His most severe punishment was to make a student walk with him during recess and lunch hour with a hand in one of his pockets, for all of the student's classmates to witness. This punishment was usually only necessary once.

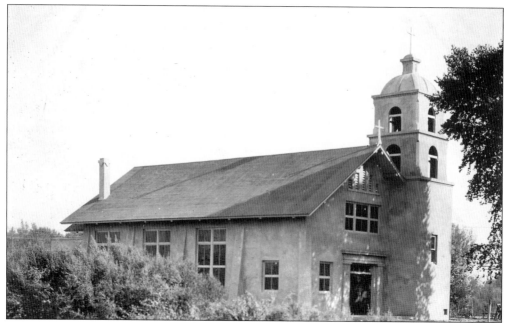

This was the first Catholic church in Blythe. In 1921, the date of this photograph, it was located on First Street between Hobsonway and Murphy Street. The current VFW Hall was the old parish hall for the church.

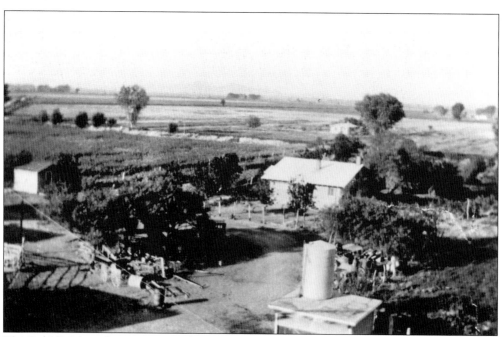

The Basil DeMeyer home is pictured in this 1922 photograph.

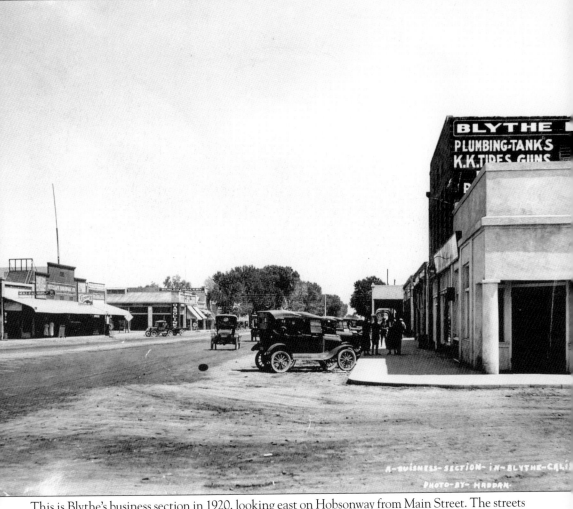

This is Blythe's business section in 1920, looking east on Hobsonway from Main Street. The streets were not paved until 1924. Note the flagpole at the intersection of Hobsonway and Broadway.

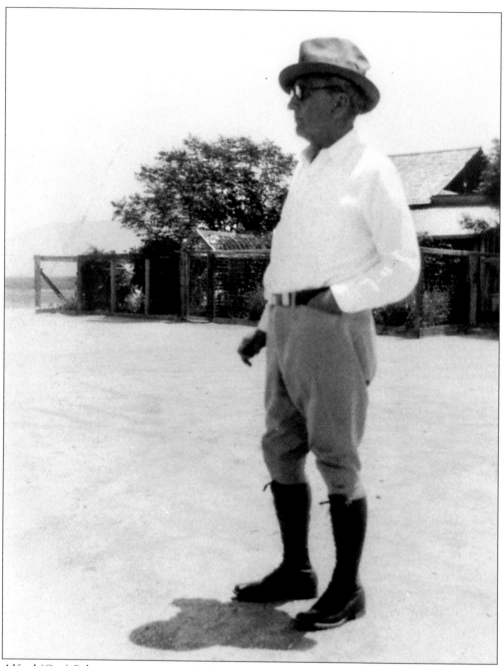

Alfred (Cap) Solano was a surveyor who laid out the Blythe townsite. He served on the first city council from 1916 to 1922 and established the Solano Club as a social center. He was also president of the Palo Verde Joint Levee District and a trustee for Palo Verde Land and Water Company.

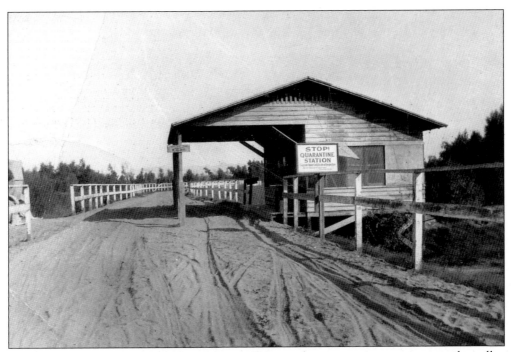

This inspection station, pictured in 1923 or 1924, was the primary entry point into the valley from Arizona.

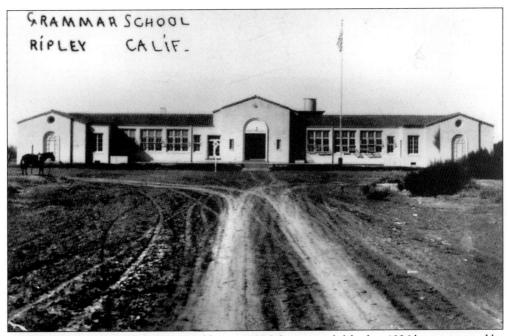

The Ripley Grammar School pictured here in 1936. It was estabilshed in 1926 but was gutted by a fire in 1935. Upon reopening in 1936, it represented the latest in modern school design.

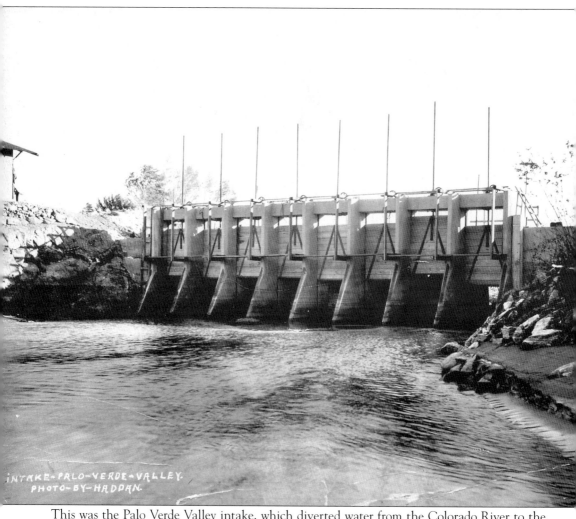

This was the Palo Verde Valley intake, which diverted water from the Colorado River to the irrigation canals.

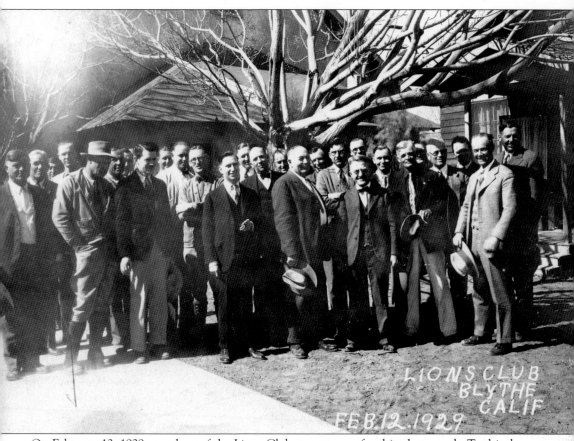

On February 12, 1929, members of the Lions Club stop to pose for this photograph. To this day, the all-men's club provides community and volunteer service in Blythe.

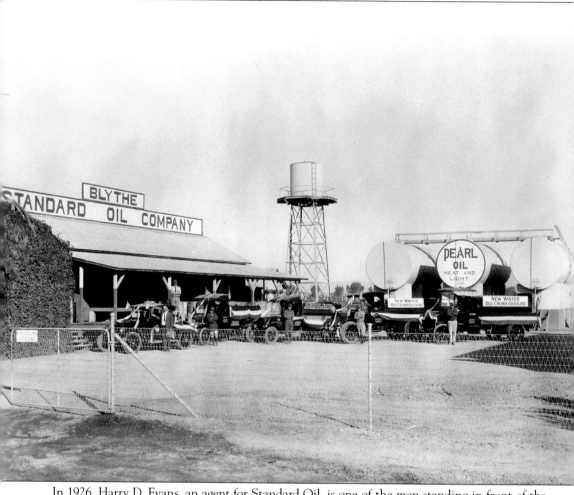

In 1926, Harry D. Evans, an agent for Standard Oil, is one of the men standing in front of the Standard Oil Company building. The others are not identified.

Three

TAMING NATURE
1930–1949

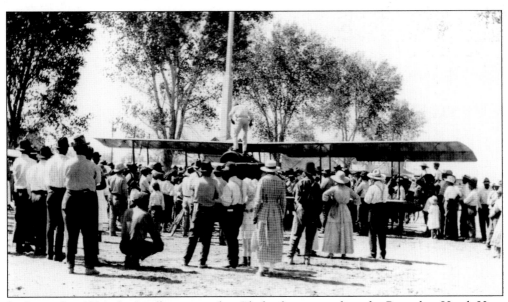

In September 1934, the Lindbergs stayed in Blythe for one week at the Bungalow Hotel. Here they are getting ready to leave the area.

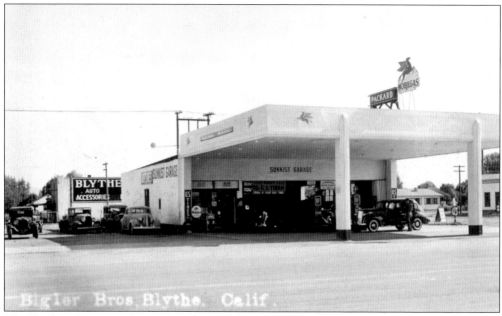

The Sunkist Garage is featured in this 1930s photograph. In the 1920s, Highway 60 through Blythe was named the Sunkist Trail by E. R. Fairbanks, a local garage operator. The title was officially used for 15 years. The Sunkist Trail stretched from Los Angeles, California, to Las Cruces, New Mexico.

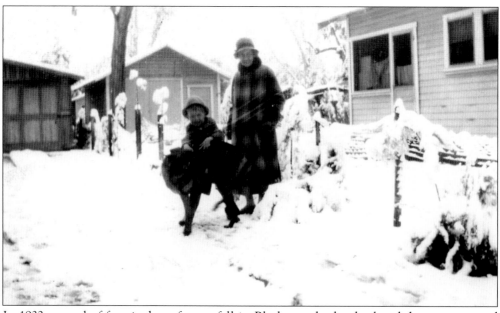

In 1932, a total of four inches of snow fell in Blythe, and schools closed due to poor road conditions. Jack Williams and his grandmother, Mrs. A. F. Masterman, pose in the snow at 160 South Broadway.

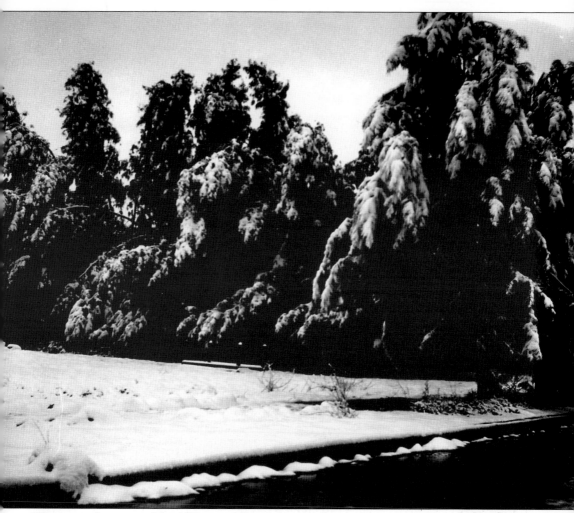

This is another view of the 1932 snowfall.

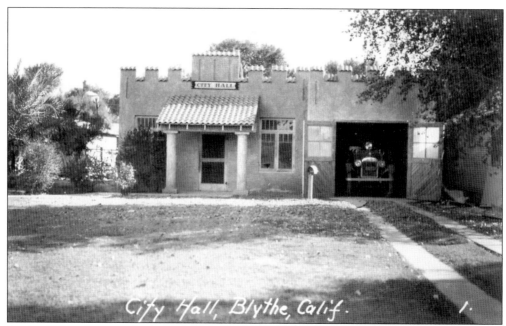

In the 1920s, this was the home of city hall and the fire station. Electricity reached Blythe in 1917. Service in the early years depended on two Snow diesel engines and power failures were frequent.

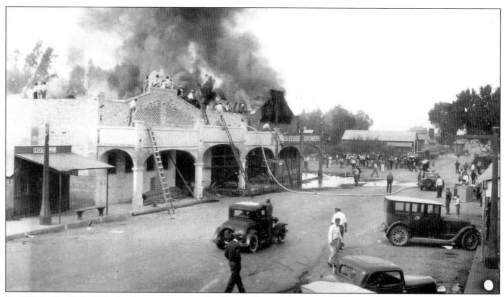

In 1933, the Palo Verde Creamery caught fire and was destroyed. It was later rebuilt. It produced butter, ice cream, milk, and eggs for local consumption. During the construction of the Metropolitan Water District's aqueduct from Parker Dam to Los Angeles, which took seven years to build, the creamery provided supplies to thousands of workers. It subsequently became the Palo Verde Ice Company plant.

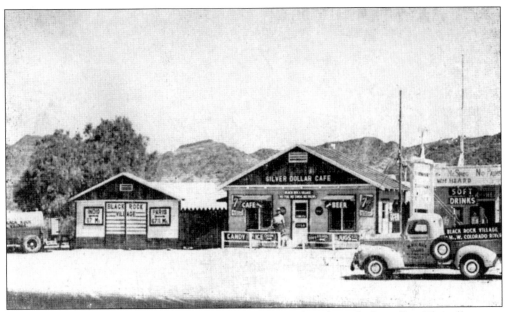

Black Rock Village was a popular stopping point for travelers through the valley. The village was on the original Highway 60-70, 10 miles west of Blythe. Nothing remains at the site.

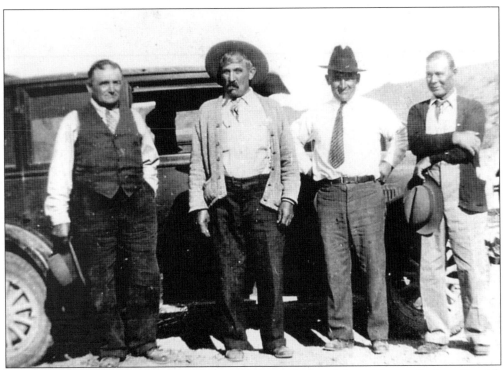

The DeMeyer brothers, pictured in this 1935 photograph, from left to right, are Isadore, Camiel, Basil, and Alidore.

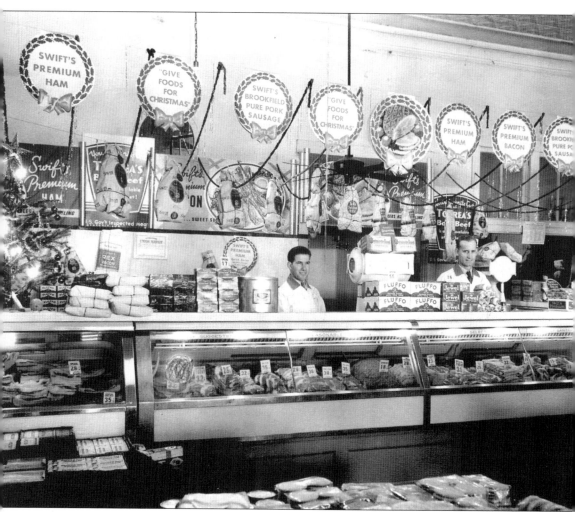

In 1935, Monroe (Butch) Ohler, left, and Robert (Bob) Manley work the meat counter at the Safeway Meat Market. Note the prices of the meat in the case.

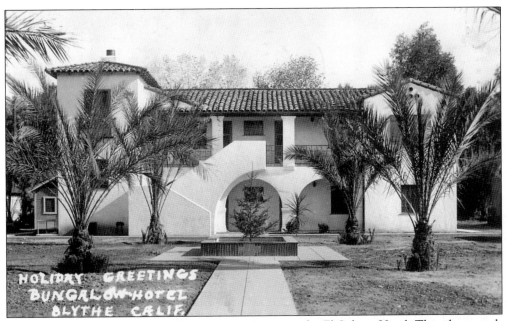

The Bungalow Hotel was a nice place to stay. It is now the El Solano Hotel. This photograph was taken before 1936.

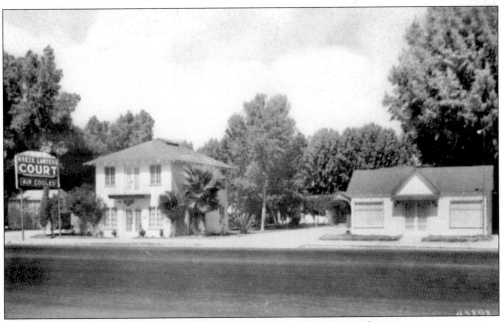

This was the Green Lantern Court. The date of the photograph is unknown.

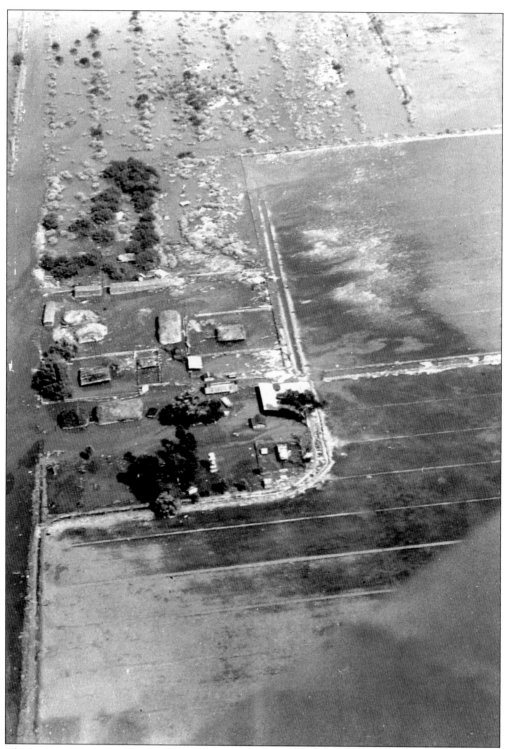

The McCoy Wash flood of 1939 was a major one in the valley. Over five inches of rain fell in a very short time causing the wash to run. The Pete Hoptman ranch, seen here, is underwater.

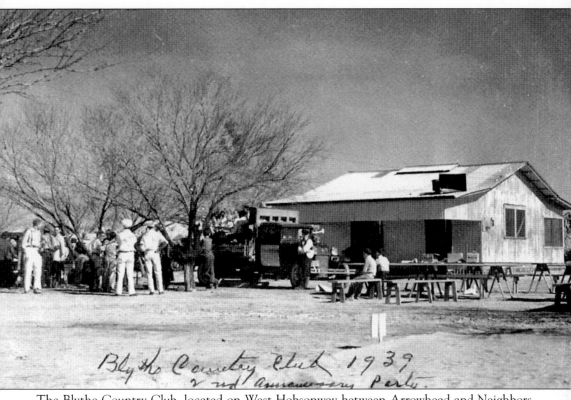

The Blythe Country Club, located on West Hobsonway between Arrowhead and Neighbors Boulevard, had a nine-hole golf course. The club is seen above in 1939.

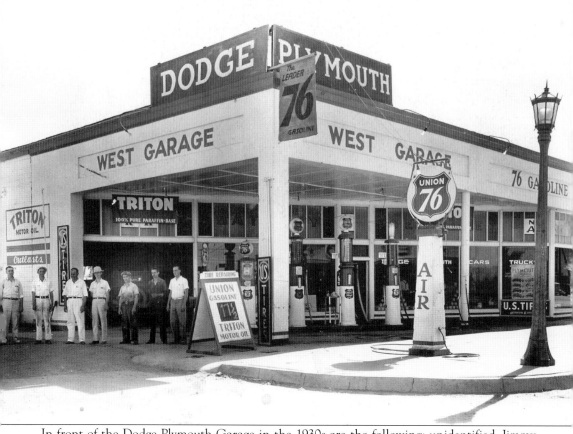

In front of the Dodge Plymouth Garage in the 1930s are the following: unidentified, Jimmy George, unidentified, Bill Sargent, O. D. Mort, and two unidentified.

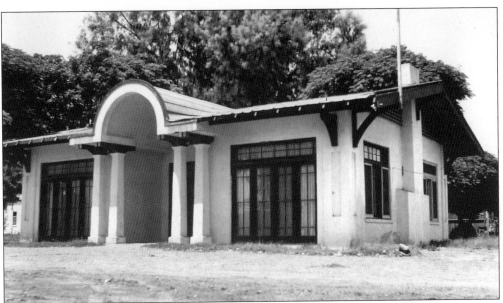

Located on North Ash Street, the American Legion Hall is seen here in the 1930s.

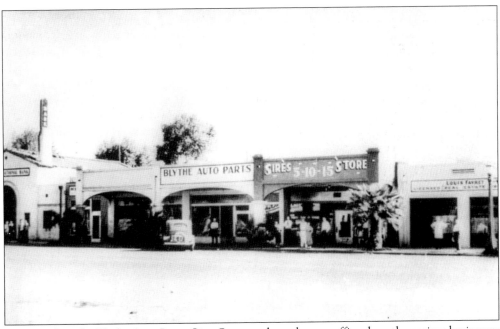

Stores such as the Blythe Auto Parts, Sires Store, and a real estate office show the various businesses and services that were available to residents in 1937.

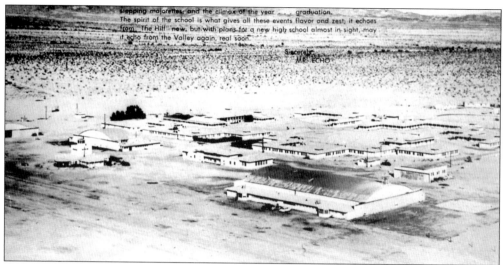

Here is a 1942 aerial view of the Morton Air Academy. This facility was run by Mr. and Mrs. Ted Morton and used to train fighter pilots during World War II. Pilots were run through the training sessions every 90 days. The school's capacity was 550 students. After World War II, Morton Air Academy was home to the beginning of the Blythe Community College. When the college moved to the high school building on Hobsonway, this facility became the high school.

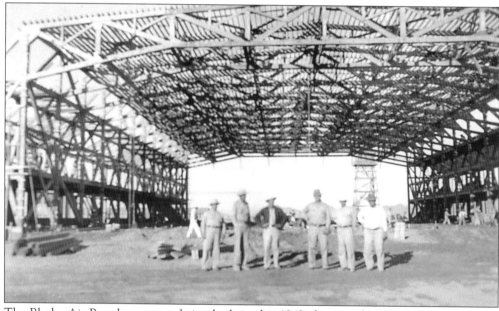

The Blythe Air Base hangar was being built in this 1942 photograph. When the air base was completed, there were 650 buildings on-site. Pictured here, from left to right, are Johnny Banks, Tex Miller, Bob Flemming, Wallis Krause, Jim Murray, and Henry Schuster. Troops were transported to the air base long before the base and permanent housing were ready. Instead they camped out in small tents in the middle of the summer when temperatures exceeded 110 degrees.

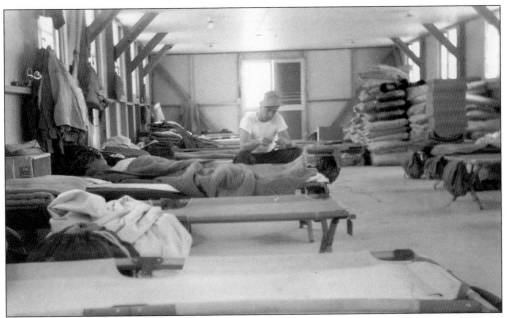

This was the Blythe Air Base barracks in 1942. The air base was home to the 390th Bomb Group during World War II. It was used to train heavy bomber crews of the Second Air Force for combat in B-17s and later B-24s. In addition to the troops stationed at the air base, some of Gen. George C. Patton's troops were stationed in the desert north of the valley, training for desert warfare. Years after the troops left the desert, local residents could go to Patton's Hill and find spent shells, tin cans, barbed wire, and other items left behind.

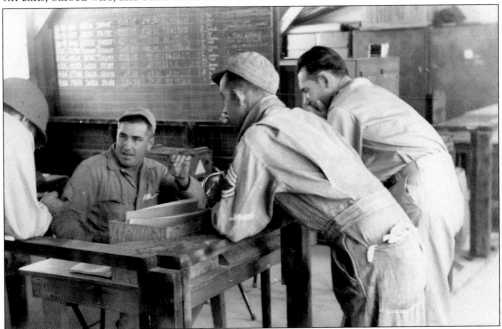

The Blythe Air Base office in 1942 is shown here. Housing for the families that accompanied the airmen to Blythe was very limited. At the time, Blythe had a population of only 4,000. Eventually war housing was provided for the military dependents.

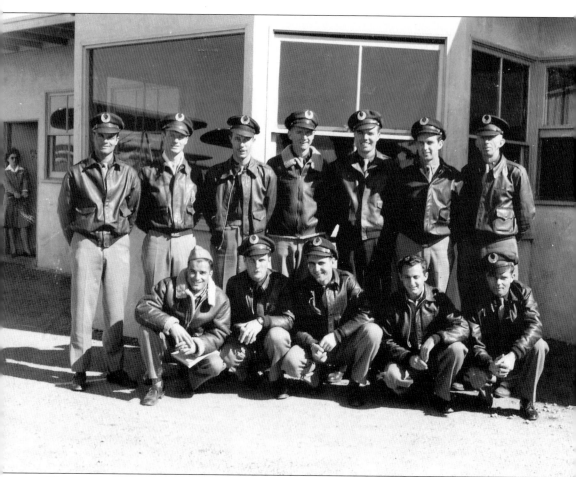

This is a photograph of Morton Air Academy graduates. Frank Zimmerman, a local resident, is pictured on the bottom row, second from the right. Frank was an instructor at the base who met and married a local girl and made Blythe his home.

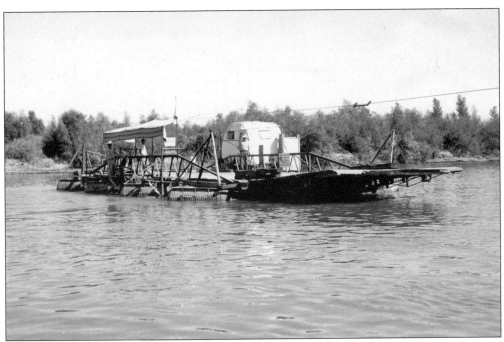

The Cibola Ferry allowed farmers in the isolated Cibola Valley, located in Arizona, southeast of Ripley, to reach civilization. The ferry carried passengers across the river until the late 1950s.

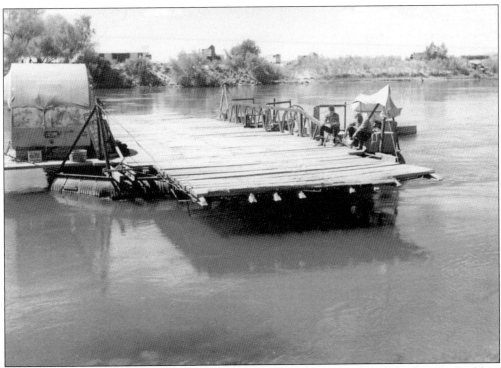

Here is another view of the Cibola Ferry. A group of ranchers replaced the ferry by building a bridge.

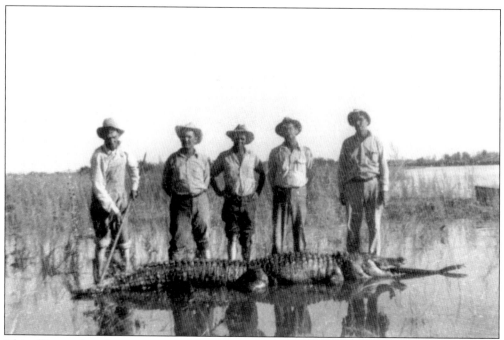

This alligator, found approximately 30 miles north of Blythe, was 10 feet long and weighed close to 500 pounds. Several explanations were given for its presence on the Colorado River. The first is that it came from an exhibition at the Santa Fe Park in Needles. The other scenario is that it was a pet of a deputy sheriff in Vidal and was set loose when the man moved away.

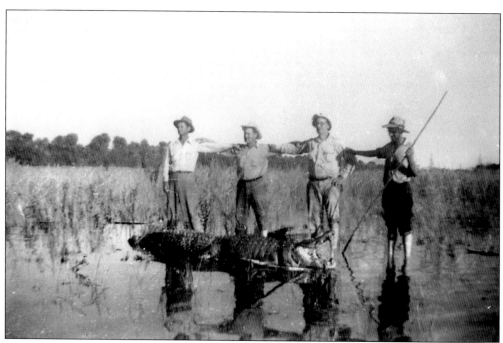

Here is another view of the alligator. Pictured, from left to right, are Ed Crook, Martin Hoover, W. H. Russell, and Ed Hoover.

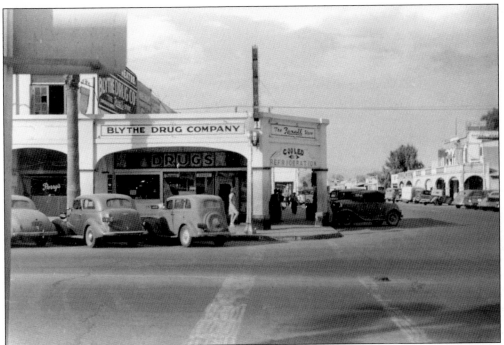

During the 1930s and 1940s, the Blythe Drug Store, seen here in 1942, also served as the Greyhound bus station. Located at the corner of Main Street and Hobsonway, the store is still in operation.

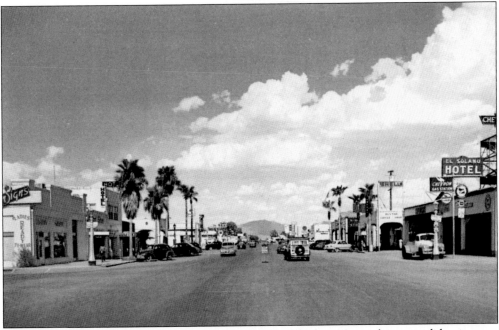

This photograph looks west on Hobsonway in Blythe. Note the varied businesses lining Hobsonway.

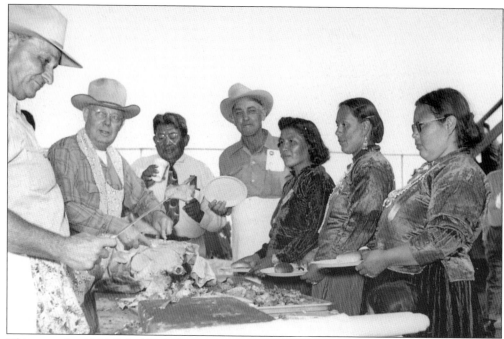

This was the 1946 Palo Verde Livestock Association rodeo grounds dedication. Pictured, from left to right, are J. K. Lofton, R. S. Williams, unidentified, Jack Marlowe, and three unidentified women.

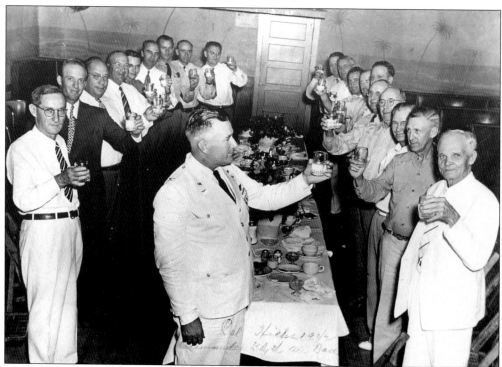

Chamber of commerce members toast Colonel Hicks, quartermaster at the Blythe Air Base, at a 1942 welcoming dinner.

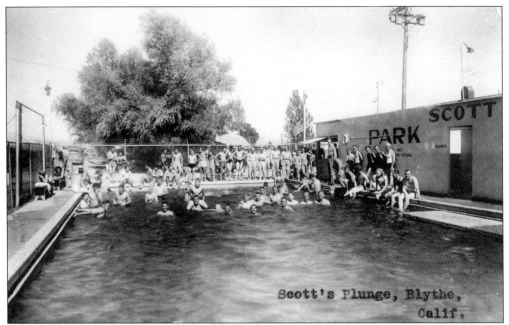

Scott's Plunge, seen in the 1940s, was the first community pool in Blythe and was located in East Blythe. It was owned and operated by George W. Scott, who was also principal of Palo Verde High School.

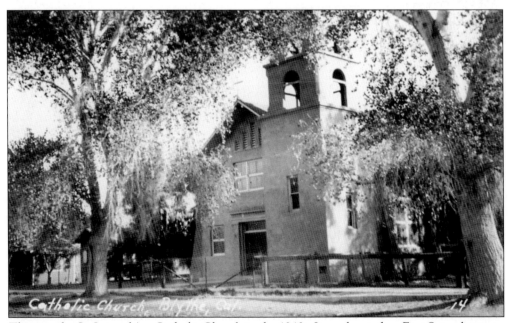

This was the St. Joan of Arc Catholic Church in the 1940s. It was located on First Street between Hobsonway and Murphy.

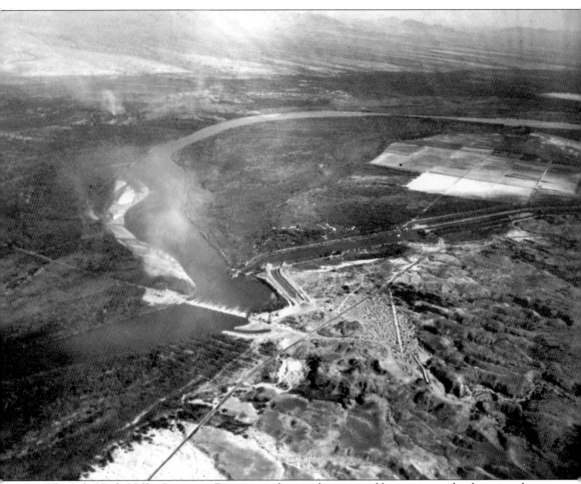

The Palo Verde Valley Irrigation District intake canal is pictured here prior to the diversion dam being built in 1959.

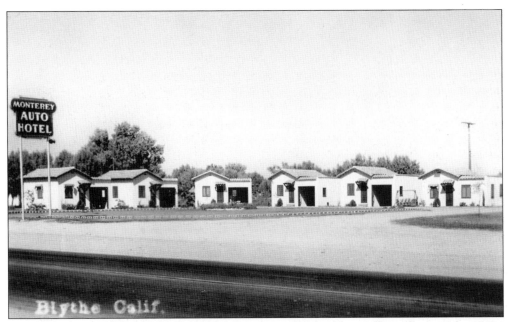

The Monterey Auto Hotel was owned by Lawrence and Helen Young. Shown here in the 1940s, it was located on the corner of Hobsonway and Third Street.

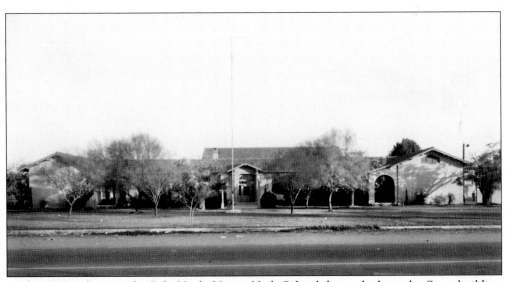

In the 1940s, this was the Palo Verde Union High School, located where the Sears building is now.

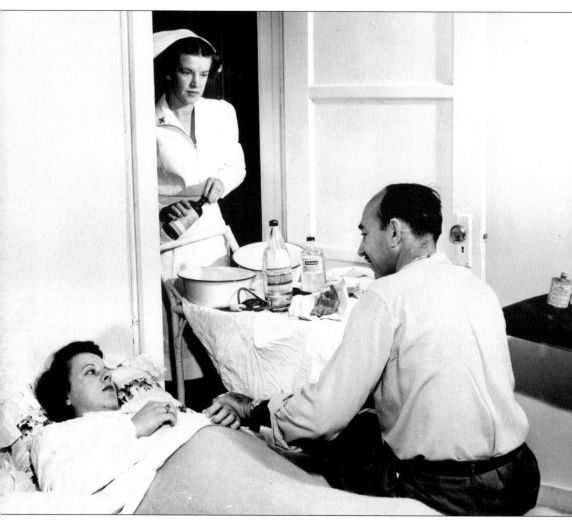

This *c.* 1948 photograph shows Dr. and Mrs. Garcia attending to an unidentified maternity patient. The hospital was actually closed at the time, as it was periodically during the 1940s and 1950s for various reasons, including lack of funds and insufficient staffing.

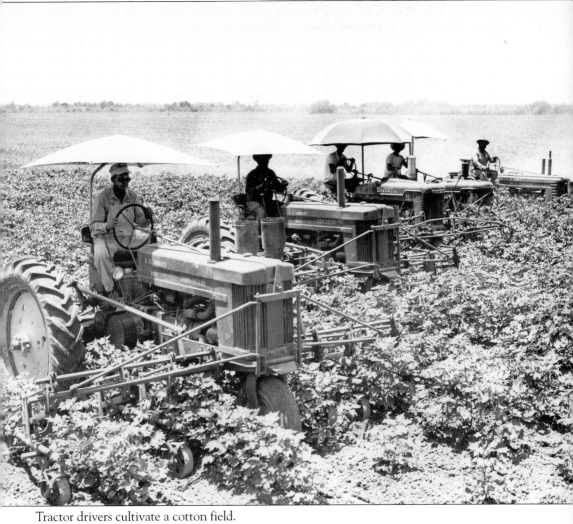

Tractor drivers cultivate a cotton field.

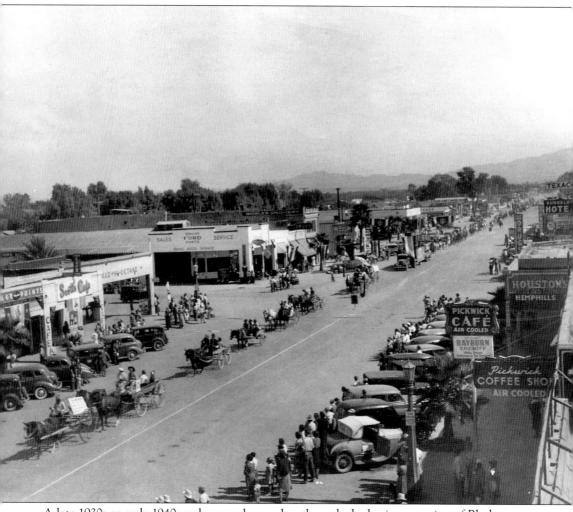

A late-1930s or early 1940s rodeo parade marches through the business section of Blythe.

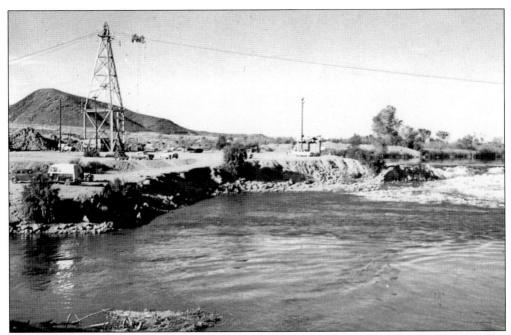

The weir was a popular fishing spot for local residents. The cable carried bucket loads of rock to build up and fortify the weir. The completion of Hoover Dam in the 1930s finally tamed the Colorado River and stopped periodic flooding.

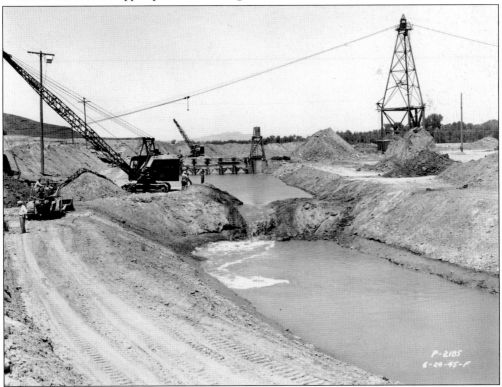

In 1945, a temporary cable way is pictured at the weir.

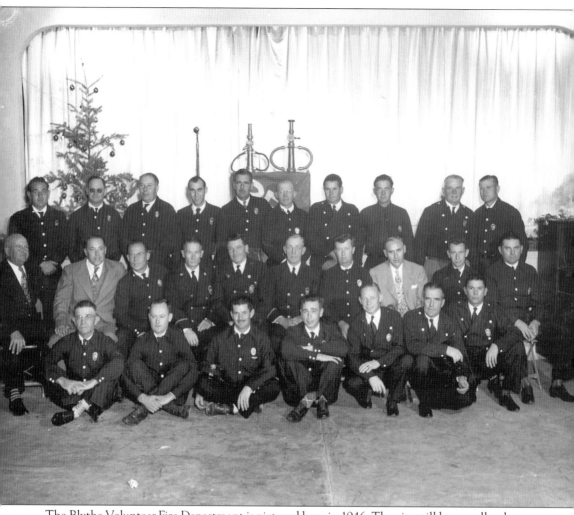

The Blythe Volunteer Fire Department is pictured here in 1946. The city still has an all-volunteer fire department.

Four

EXPANSION
1950–1979

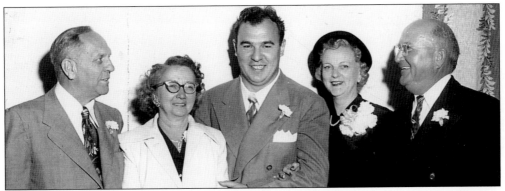

Present at a community function, from left to right, are California governor Knight, Florence Balz, Angie Alexander, Mrs. Knight, and Bill Balz.

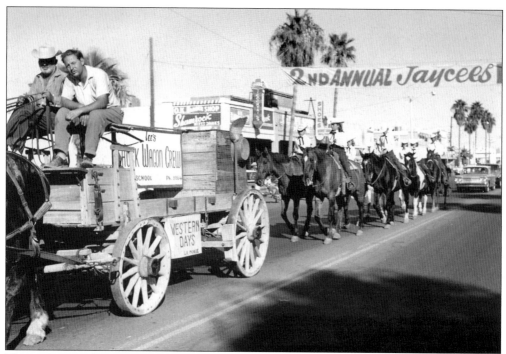

The 2nd Annual Jaycee Rodeo parade travels through Blythe in 1958. The man in the wagon with the beard is L. A. Morse. Following the wagon is the Blythe Teenage Quadrille.

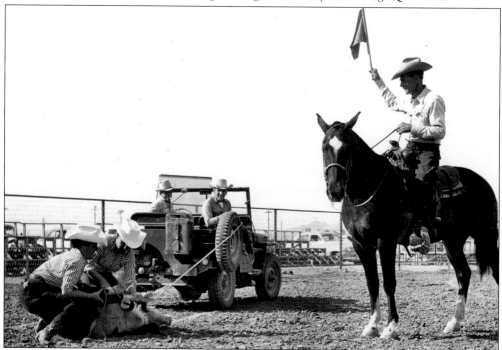

This 1950s photograph of the Blythe Riding Club Women's Stampede shows one of the events— jeep roping. Pictured, from left to right, are Eva LaVoy, Katie Gossett, Frenchie LaVoy, Rusty Burkett, and Warren Higgens.

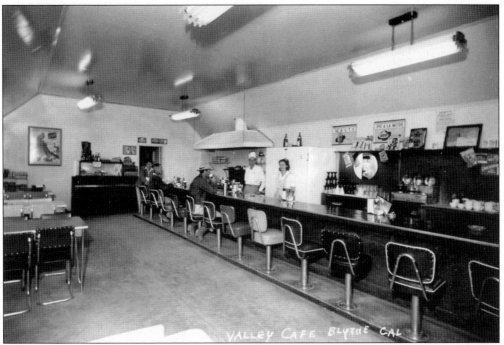

The Valley Cafe in Balzberg was owned by Mac McDaniel. This photograph was taken in the early 1950s.

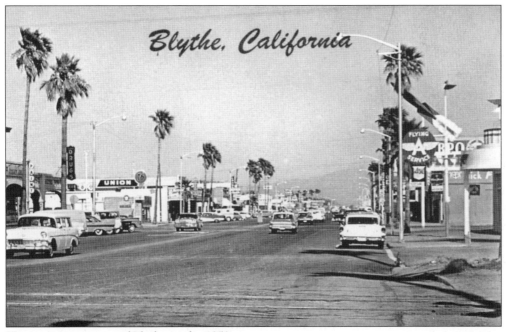

Here is a street scene of Blythe in the 1950s.

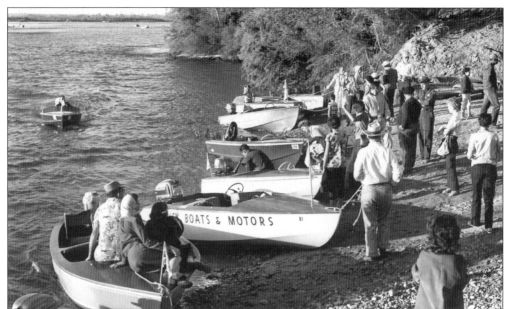

This is a photograph of the Blythe Boat Cruise in the mid-1950s. The route went from Blythe, south to Lake Martinez, and returned the following day. The Blythe Boat Club started this yearly event as a tourist attraction to introduce outsiders to the Colorado River and bring business to Blythe. It stopped for several years when there were not enough men willing to be river pilots, but the cruise has recently been revived due to the efforts of Mike McDowell. It is once again an annual event held in May.

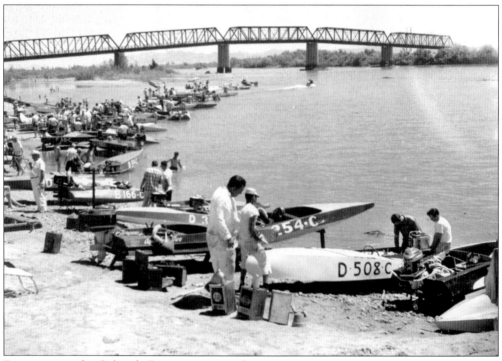

Boat races on the Colorado River were a popular event.

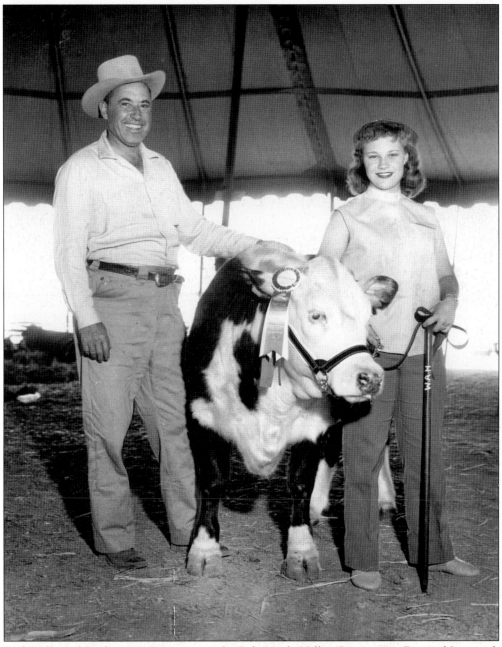
Bud Wells and Darlene McCain pose at the Palo Verde Valley Community Fair and Livestock Show in the late 1950s with McCain's champion steer.

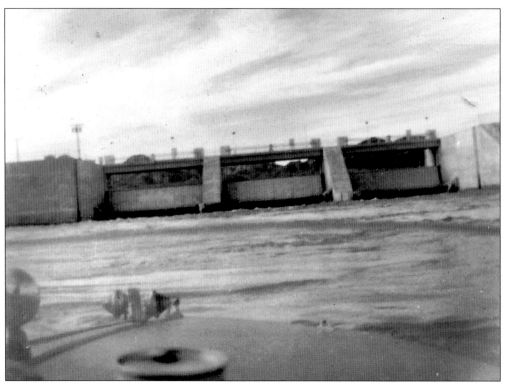

In 1959, this diversion dam replaced the old rock weir.

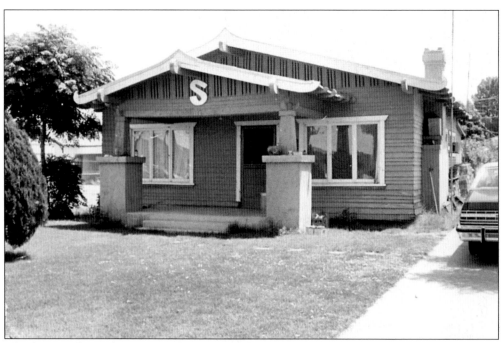

This house is located at 144 South Palm. The house was built in the early 1920s by one of the Barlow Brothers, using Chinese labor. Note the oriental influence on the front of the house.

Colis S. Mayflower is shown in this 1950 photograph being honored by the Masons. He came to Blythe in 1932 and was the mayor in 1937, 1938, and 1943. He was also chairman of the Palo Verde Irrigation District Board of Directors. He was the moving force for the construction of a new airport terminal after he was elected to the Riverside County Board of Supervisors in 1949. Mayflower County Park at Sixth Avenue and the river are named after him.

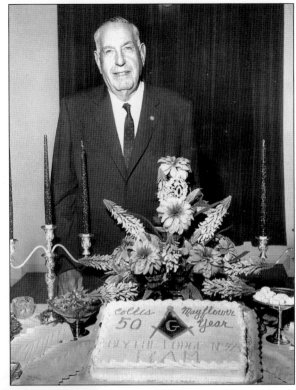

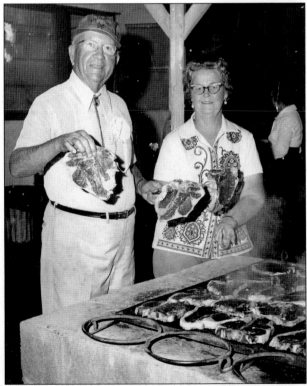

Bill Balz and Fern Fallowfield are shown here at a barbecue in the 1950s. Bill Balz came to Blythe in 1937. He subdivided the Garrison Tract, one of the first housing divisions in Blythe. He also subdivided 80 acres just west of the city limits into a development known as Balzberg. He was instrumental in raising funds to remodel the hospital and was the founder of the first Blythe Country Club. Fern Fallowfield and her husband, Irving, co-owned the Blythe Drug Store with D. C. "Johnnie" Johnson.

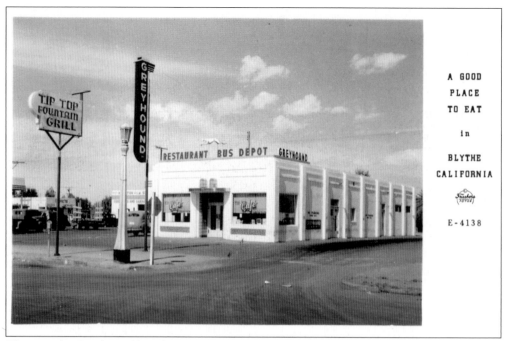

This was the Greyhound bus depot in the 1950s.

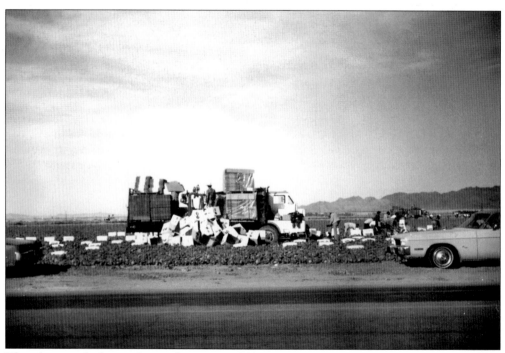

This photograph shows a lettuce harvest in 1983.

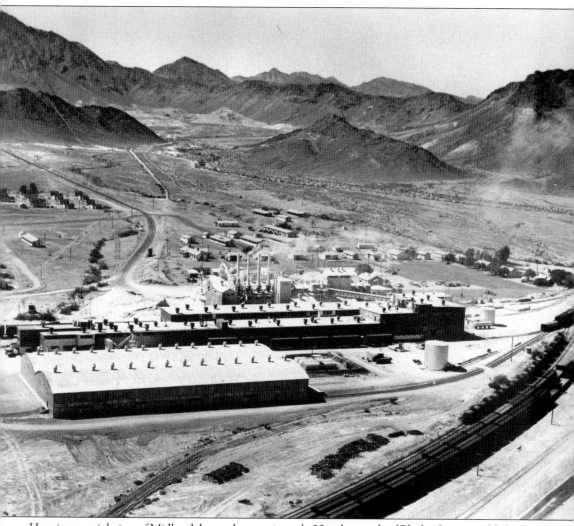

Here is an aerial view of Midland, located approximately 20 miles north of Blythe. It was established in 1915 and was originally known as Mineral City. The company town existed to provide services to the gypsum mine workers. The mine closed in 1966, and many of the structures were moved to Blythe. The mining rights were originally owned by Floyd Brown and were sold to American Gypsum in 1911.

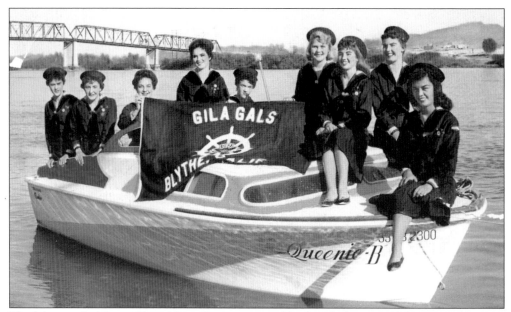

The Mariner Girl Scout Troup No. 116 was sponsored by the Blythe Boat Club. Pictured here on March 8, 1959, from left to right, are Kay Mitchell, Pat Matlock, Susan Lewis, Diana Feemster, Norma Owens, Valerie Johnson, Zora Marshall, Susan Sanders, and Bea Sevilla.

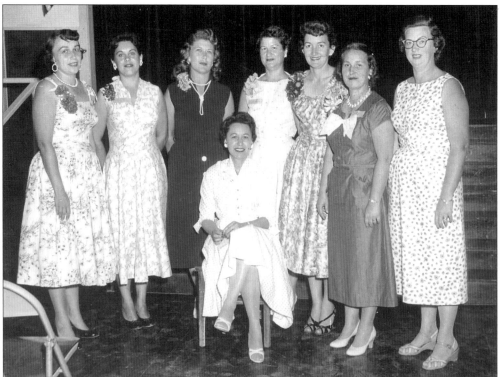

This is the Parent Teacher Association installation of officers. Pictured here in the late 1950s or early 1960s, from left to right, are Camille Boehning, Shirley Dekens, Jean Hughes, Emilie Graham, Ruby Browning, Barbara Brugh, and Pat Sain. Seated in front is Mary Tatosian.

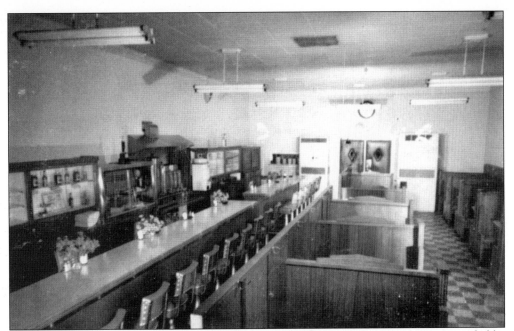

In 1936, the Blythe Coffee Shop opened. The postcard advertises that it was recommended by Duncan Hines. This photograph was taken in the early 1950s.

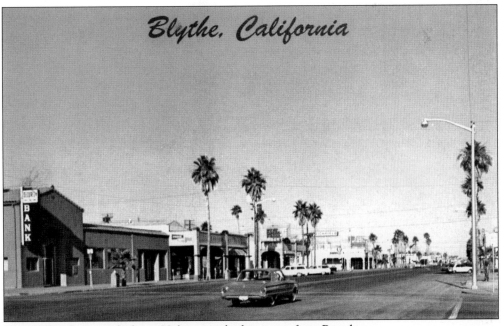

This 1950s photograph shows Hobsonway looking west from Broadway.

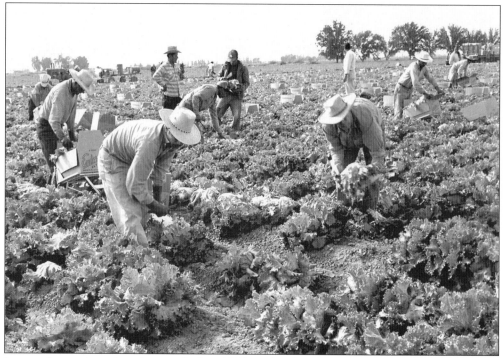

Lettuce harvesting takes place in the late 1950s at this farm.

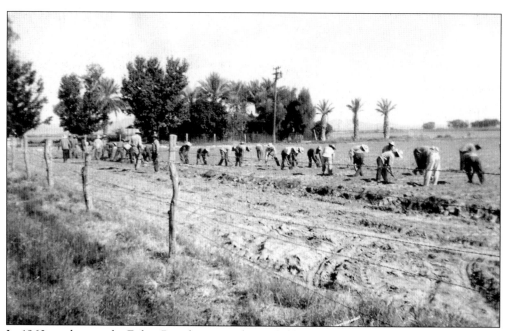

In 1960, workers at the Fisher Ranch are weeding a field.

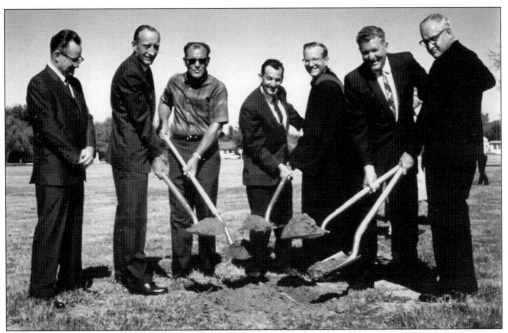

At the groundbreaking ceremony in January 1966 for the Community United Methodist Church, from left to right, are three unidentified, Frank Zimmerman, Bon Brummet, Clark Browning, and Joe Gleeson. The Felix Applebee Grammar School previously stood on this site.

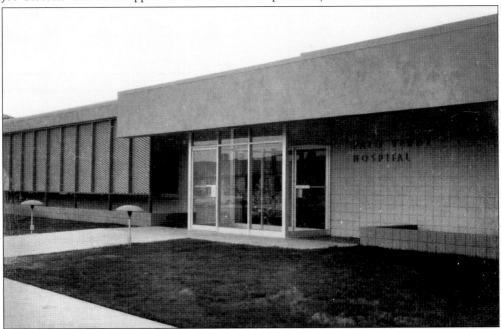

Above is the addition to Palo Verde Hospital, completed in 1981 to give the facility 19 more beds. The hospital came into existence in 1925, when the American Legion donated its clubhouse to be used as a hospital. In 1937, the hospital moved to its present site on North First Street. It was closed off and on during the early years. The Palo Verde Hospital Association was formed in 1948 and expanded the bed capacity to 24.

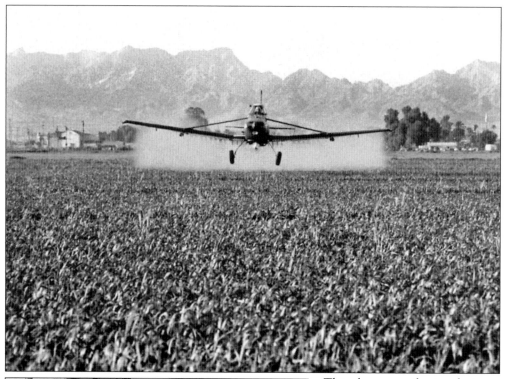

This plane, crop dusting during the 1970s, belongs to West Coast Flying Service.

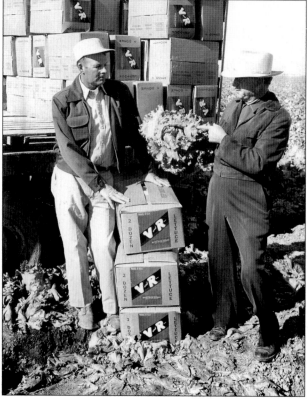

Tom Vosses and Clarence Robinson inspect lettuce during a lettuce harvest in the 1950s. They were partners in Blythe Melon Growers. Upon Vosses death in 1961, Clarence bought his share and the company became known as Robinson Farms. Robinson Farms is still in existence today and is owned and operated by his wife, Marie, and their children Danny Robinson and Betty Blackwood.

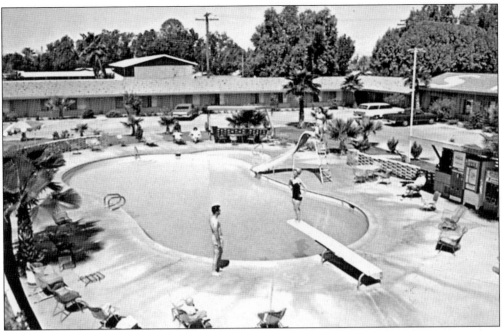

This is the Sahara Motor Hotel in the 1970s. One of the first motels in Blythe to have a swimming pool, it opened in 1964.

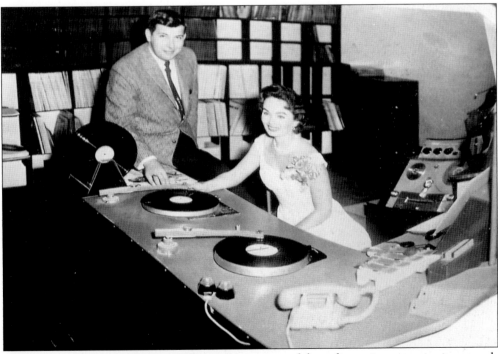

Actress Ann Blythe and Richard Whitcomb, manager of the radio station, are spinning records in the studio during the 1960s.

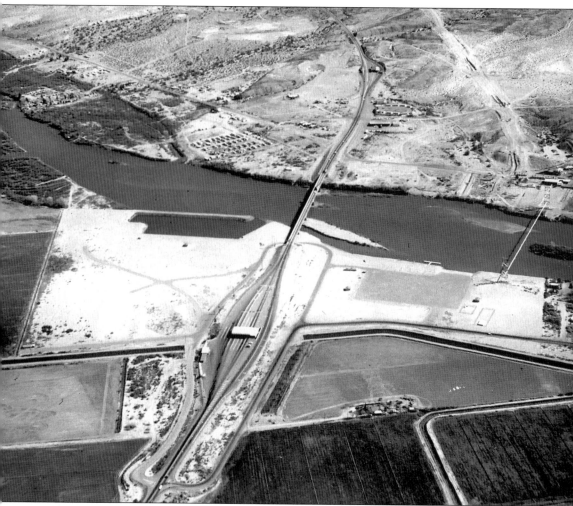

This is a 1968 aerial view of Interstate 10 looking east towards Arizona. The interstate was finished in 1965.

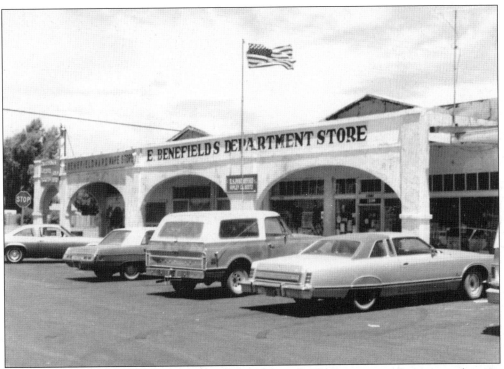

Built in 1919 by the Southern California Railroad, Benefield's Department Store, seen above in 1987, burned down in May 1992.

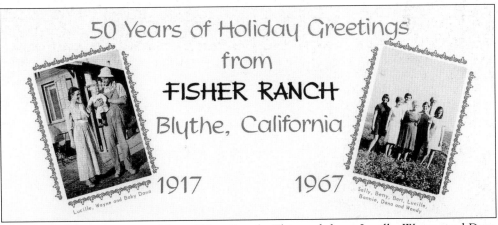

This is a holiday greeting card from Fisher Ranch. This card shows Lucille, Wayne, and Dana Fisher in 1917, and Sally, Betty, Bart, Lucille, Bonnie, Dana, and Wendy Fisher in 1967. Fisher Ranch was founded in 1917 and was the first ranch in the valley to raise Brahma cattle. Dana Fisher, born and raised in the valley, was an outstanding farmer and was given the Howie Award by the Riverside County Farm Bureau. The Fisher Ranch, one of the largest farming operations in the valley, is still in operation and is currently managed by Bart Fisher, the grandson of Wayne and Lucille Fisher.

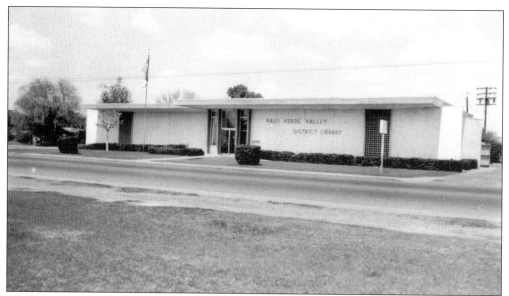

The Palo Verde District Library Association was formed in 1959 and, in 1960, the Palo Verde Valley Library was built. It is located on the corner of Broadway and Chanslorway. The first library was established in 1914 and was located in a small building next to the post office. In 1928, it was moved to the Little Brown Church. It had several more homes before it finally obtained its permanent one shown here.

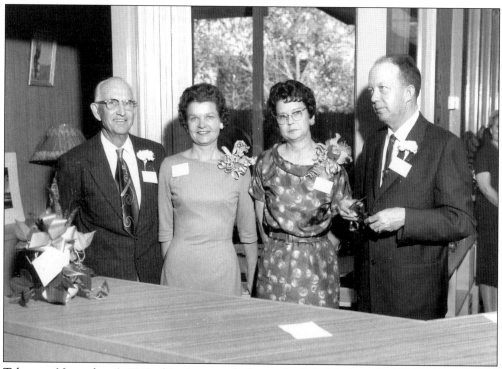

Taken on November 6, 1960, this photograph shows the Palo Verde Valley Library dedication. Pictured, from left to right, are Dale Braman, Margaret Port, Bea Waggoner, and Grady Setzler.

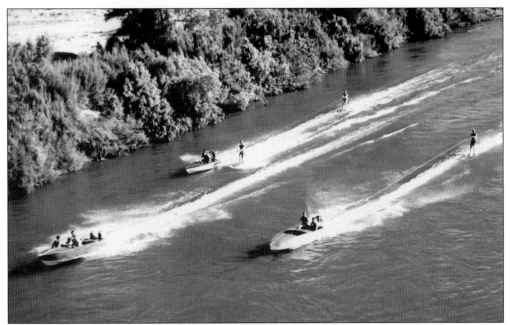

Recreation on the Colorado River has always been an important part of life in the valley, as evidenced by this late-1950s or early 1960s photograph.

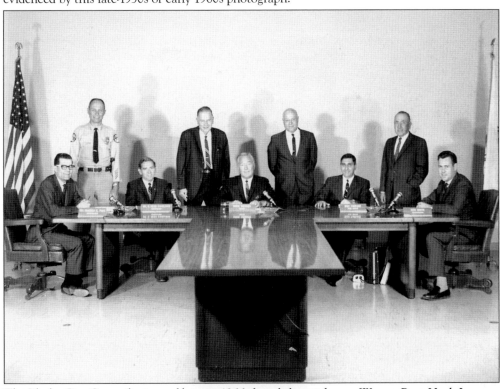

The Blythe City Council, pictured here in 1966, from left to right, are Warren Port, Hugh Ingram, Reed Eshelman, Arthur Cusick, Veryl Bommer, Robert Brockmier, Dick Farrage, Bud Wells, and Harold Fischer.

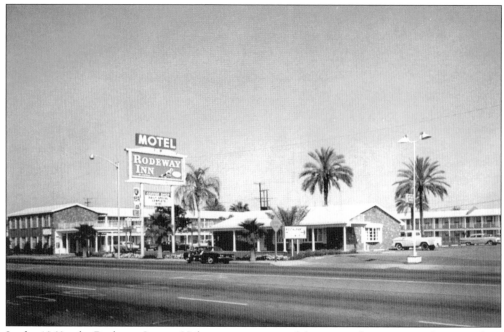

In the 1960s, the Rodeway Inn on Hobsonway was one of the nicest places to stay when traveling through the valley.

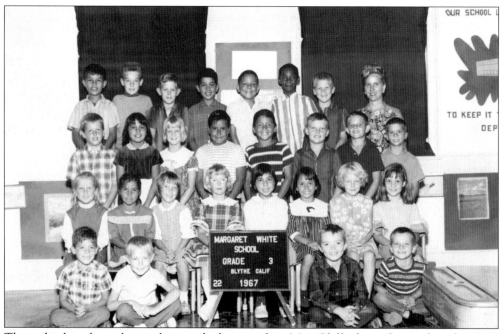

These third-grade students, along with their teacher, Mrs. Clifford, are featured in this 1967 Margaret White School class photograph.

Five

MODERN TIMES
1980–PRESENT

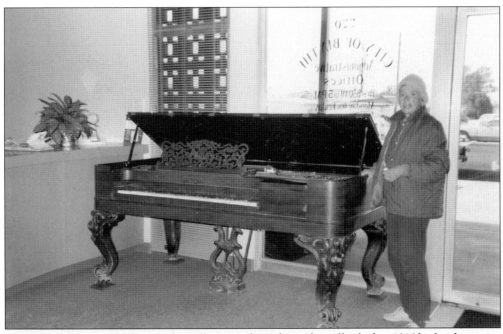

The 1874 Steinway grand piano shown here was brought to the valley before 1916 by freight wagon from Glamis. The owners, Mr. and Mrs. Carrigan, died in the influenza epidemic of 1918. Herman Neipp later donated the piano to the primary school. After World War II, the piano was moved to the high school on the mesa. Mary Davenport, pictured here, bought the piano in 1951 and donated it to the museum in 1987. It is currently on display at the museum.

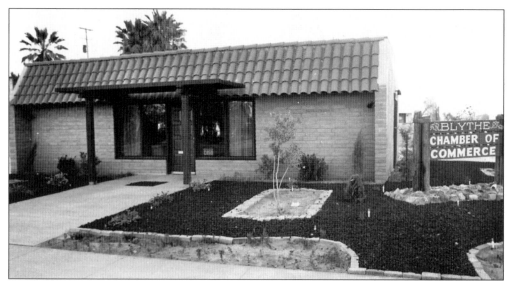

The current Blythe Chamber of Commerce building was built in 1984 on South Broadway. Established in 1911, the chamber of commerce continues to promote the activities of the Palo Verde Valley. Each year, they host the Colorado River Country Music Festival, Economic Outlook Conference, and the Jazz Festival.

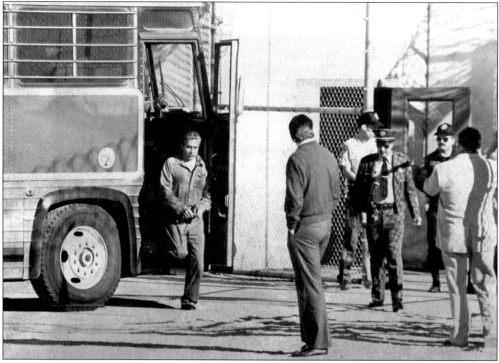

On December 1, 1988, Chuckawalla Valley State Prison opened, approximately 18 miles west of Blythe. This photograph shows the first inmate to arrive at the prison. A second prison, Ironwood State Prison, opened in 1993 adjacent to Chuckawalla. The prisons currently house over 8,000 inmates and employ over 1,600 people. During the prison site selection process, a bus full of local residents went to Sacramento to support the prison being built here.

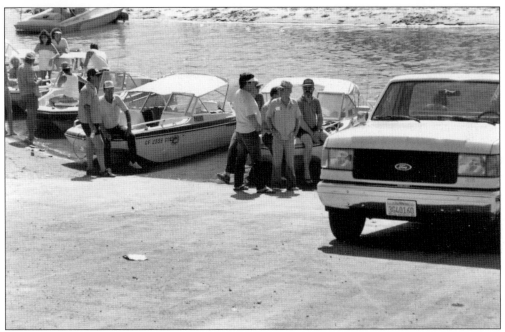

Boats are launching for the 1988 Blythe River Cruise, originally called the Blythe Boat Cruise. The boats head south to Martinez Lake, where everyone spent the night and returns to Blythe the next day.

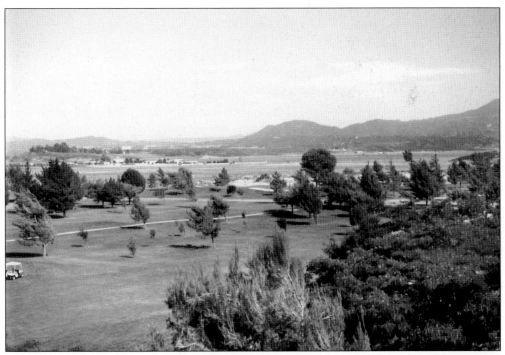

Blythe Municipal Golf Course, located on the mesa north of the valley, has spectacular views of the surrounding area. Pictured here in 1983, the 18-hole golf course draws many winter visitors to the valley.

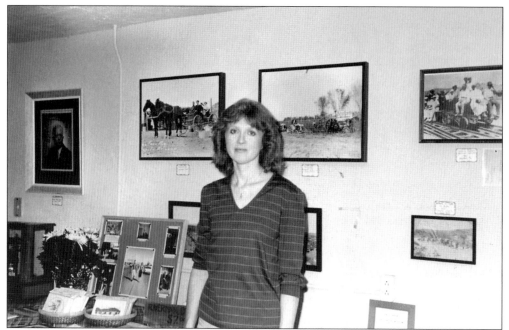

Nancy Graham was the first president of the Palo Verde Historical Museum and Society. She currently lives in Santa Barbara, California. She is married to Richard "Dick" Graham, son of Charlie and Emilie Graham, longtime residents of the valley.

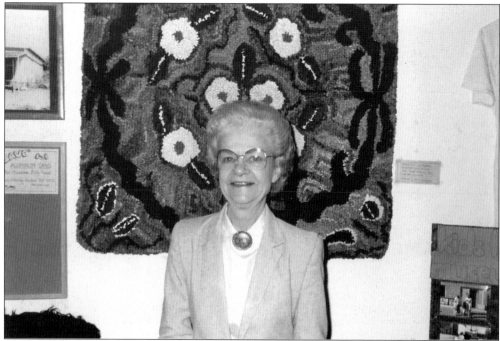

Margaret Port, shown here in 1989, was a founding member of the museum and served as president of the board of directors until 1996. She and her husband, Warren R. Port, donated a building to the Palo Verde Historical Museum allowing the museum to display its artifacts. Mrs. Port also served on the board of directors of the cemetery district and library district.

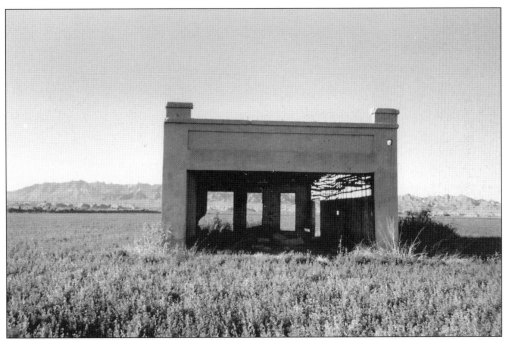

Pictured in 1990, these are the remains of the Fertilla Store, which was located on North Lovekin between Sixth and Fourth Avenues.

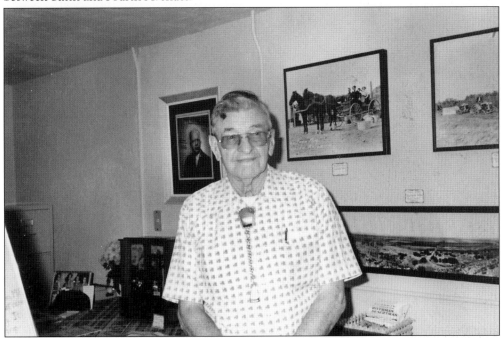

Sarhas Dekens, seen here in 1984, came to Blythe in 1908 at the age of nine. He was the fire chief from 1941 until he retired in 1966. He also served on the Blythe City Council for 10 years. He was a charter member of the Lions Club, a member of the Knights of Columbus for 50 years, and served on the board of directors for the cemetery district for 29 years. His family is still prominent in the valley.

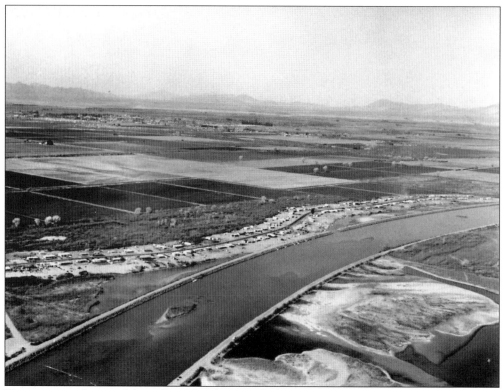

Here is an aerial view of the valley. The photograph shows the Riviera Drive development, south of Interstate 10.

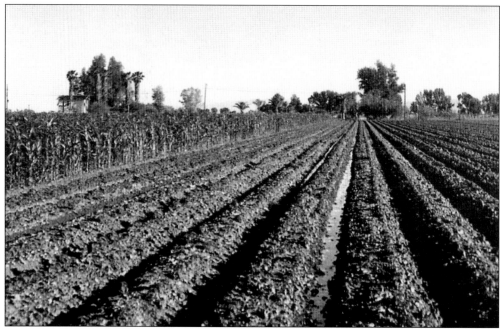

The farming of cotton and corn in the valley can be seen above. The climate and availability of water make this valley one of the most productive in the nation.

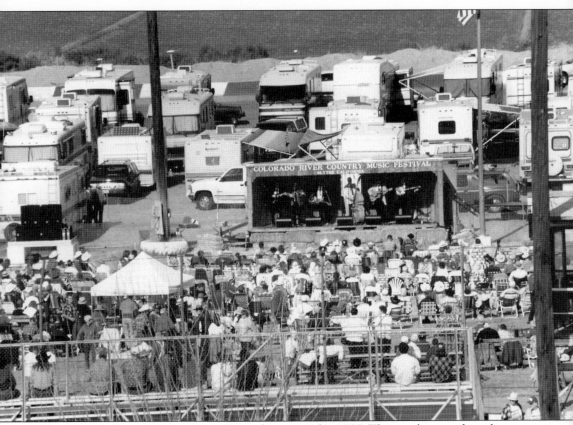

The Colorado River Country Music Festival is pictured in 1998. This yearly event draws between 10,000 and 20,000 visitors to the valley from all over the United States and Canada.

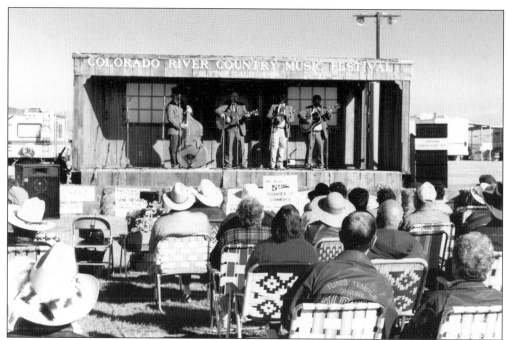

Pictured here in 1998 at the Colorado River Country Music Festival is a band called the Colorado River Boys. From left to right, they are Bryan Adams, Doc Cheatwood, David Mort, and Francis Rodriguez.

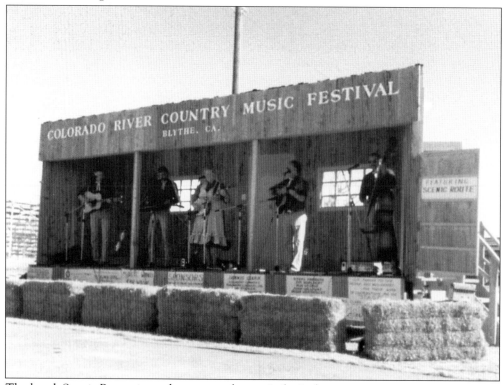

The band, Scenic Route, is on the stage at the music festival.

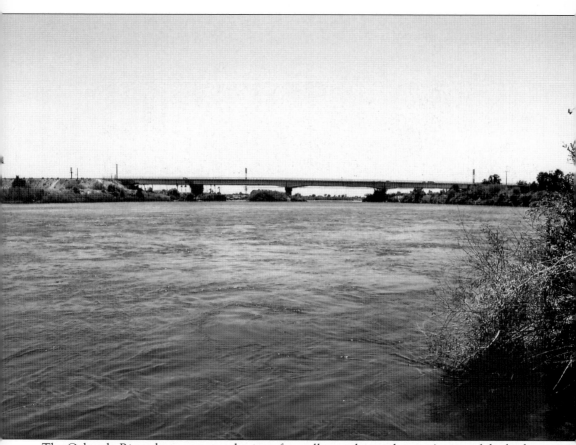

The Colorado River draws water enthusiasts from all over the southwest. A view of the bridge over the river is seen in 2005.

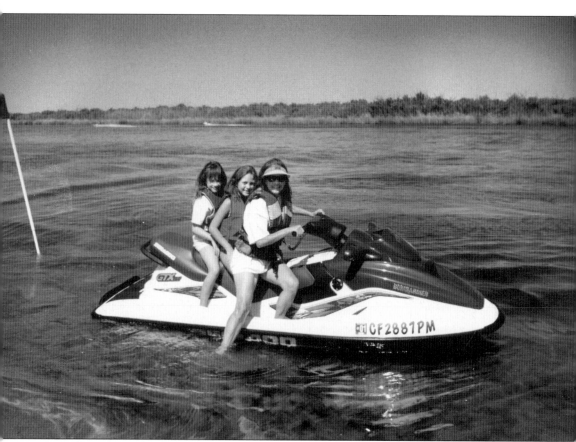

Juana Iroz, Angie Harkinson, and Cassandra Iroz-Bryce enjoy jet skiing on the water. This photograph was taken in 2000 at the Blythe Boat Club, 13 miles north of Blythe.

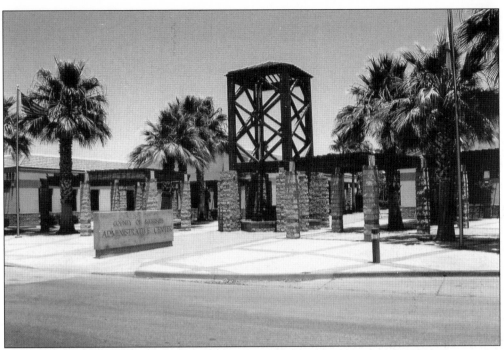

This is the Riverside County Administrative Center. This complex opened in 1998.

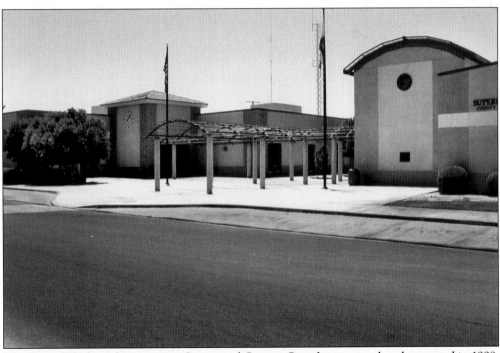

The City of Blythe Administrative Center and County Courthouse complex also opened in 1998.

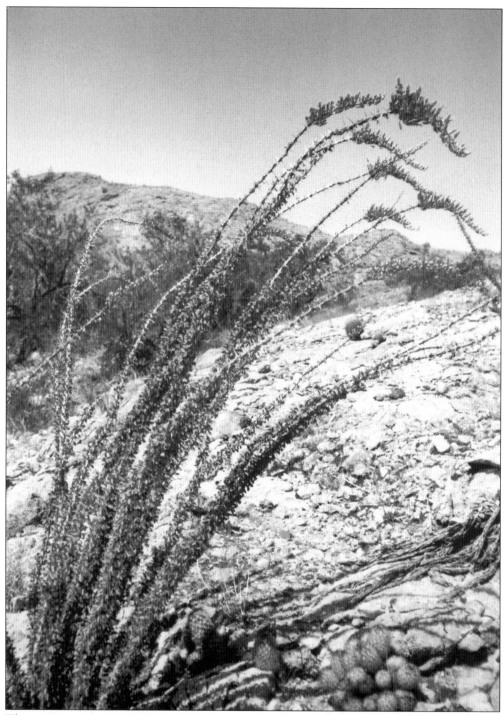

The spring rains of 1983 were abundant, and the desert was beautiful. Pictured here is an ocotillo: a thorny, scarlet-flowered candlewood.

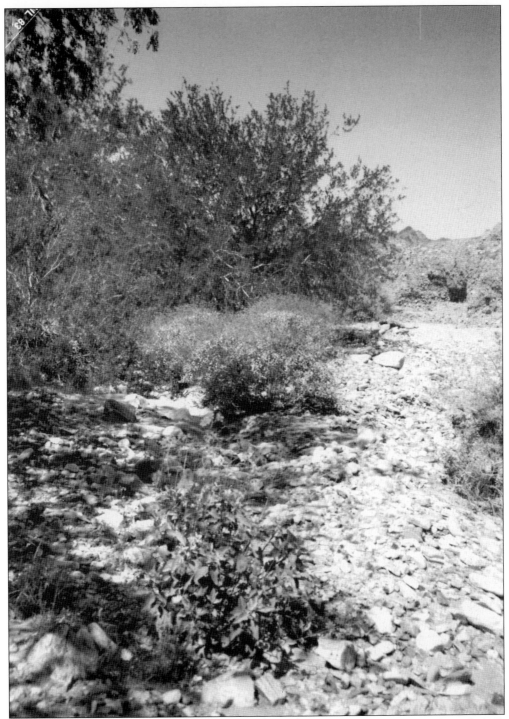

Here are more blossoms in 1983. The desert area around the Palo Verde Valley abounds with ocotilla, ironwood, mesquite catclaw (a yellow-flowered spiny acacia), sagebrush, as well as coyotes, bobcats, skunks, foxes, rattlesnakes, deer, and bighorn sheep, to name a few. After a rainy winter and spring, wildflowers of all descriptions crop up in the summer and fall.

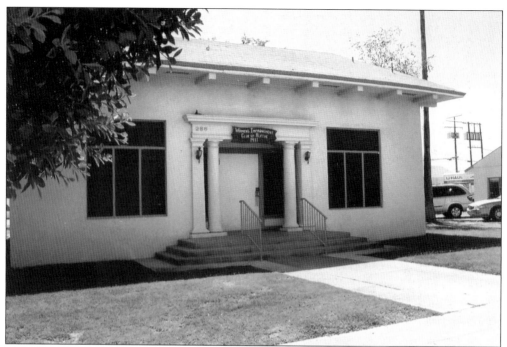

The Blythe Women's Improvement Club, shown in 2005, was built in 1911. During the 1990s, it was refurbished and continues to serve as the home for the Women's Improvement Club and the Junior Women's Improvement Club of Blythe.

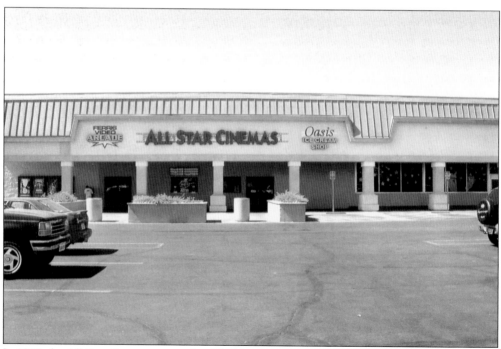

In 1997, the All Star Cinemas opened in Blythe. The valley was without a cinema for many years after the Hub Theater closed.

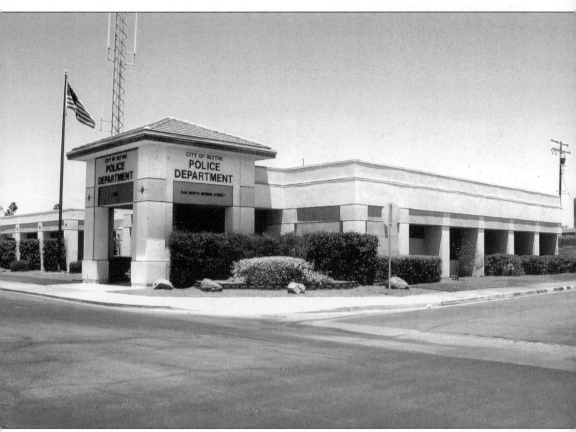

This is the City of Blythe Police Department in 2005. Its modern appearance and police force are a far cry from the original. Walter Walsh was the first town marshal in 1916 and was paid $20 per month.

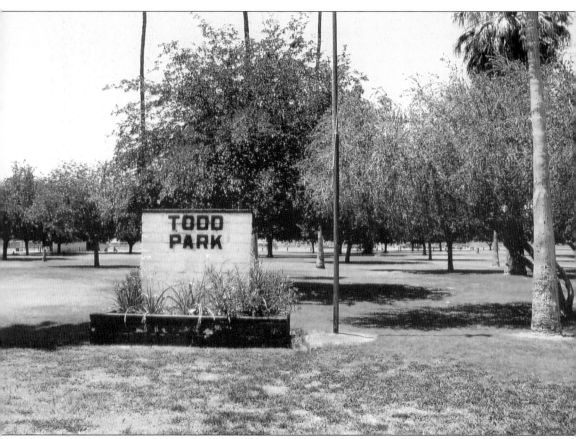

Named after L. B. "Bert" Todd, who came to the valley in 1903, Todd Park occupies a full city block in the center of town. Bert Todd and his brothers operated a well drilling business. In 1916, he purchased the old Electric Theater, expanded it, and later operated it as the Liberty Theatre. In addition to building a fenced-in baseball diamond at the park, he also helped build a small library for the town.

In 1995, Gary and Angie Harkinson enjoy the merry-go-round at the Colorado River Country Fair.

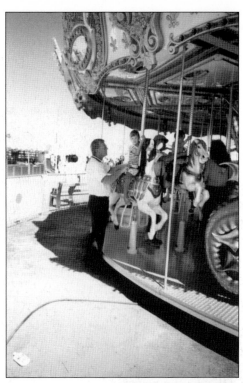

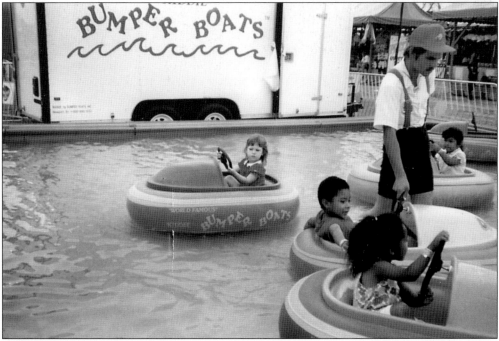

Children enjoy bumper boats at the Colorado River Country Fair in 1994. In addition to the fair, the annual Junior Livestock auction is held at the same time. Children raise rabbits, fowl, sheep, pigs, goats, and cattle as part of their 4-H activities during the year. Recent auctions have raised over $300,000.

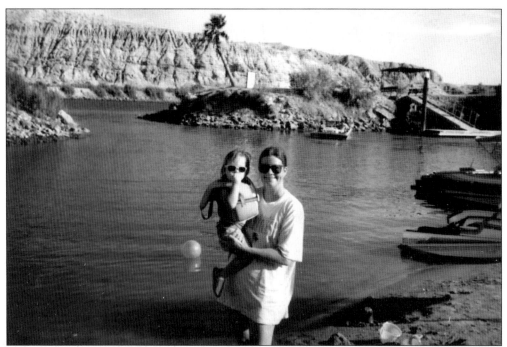

The river is a great place to hang out. Shown in 1993 are Marilee and Angie Harkinson at McIntyre Park. Marilee is the daughter of Warren and Margaret Port.

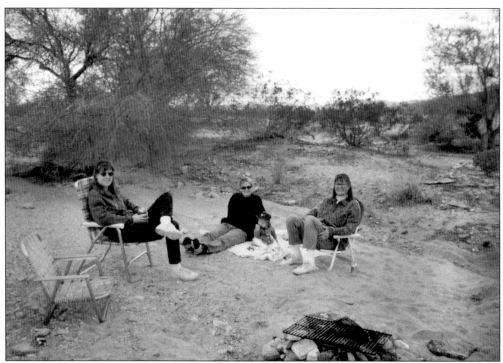

Pictured here at a desert picnic in 1998, from left to right, are Jenny Cyr, Kerin Port, Phoebe Cyr, and Sally Morgan.

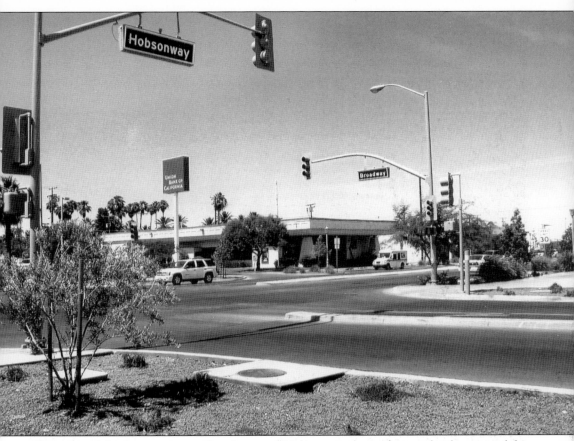

This view of the intersection at Broadway and Hobsonway shows the new landscaping of the downtown area, which was completed in 2004.

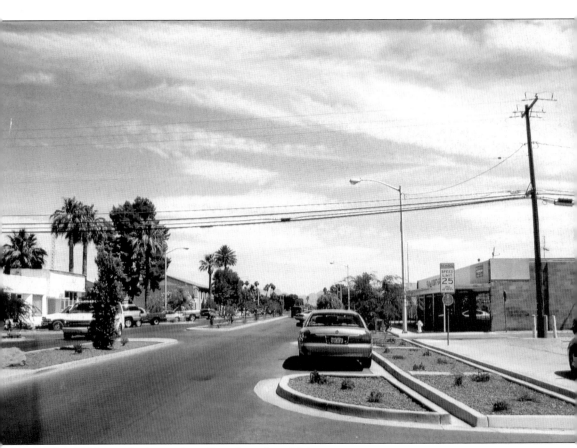

This 2005 view looks north on Broadway from Hobsonway.

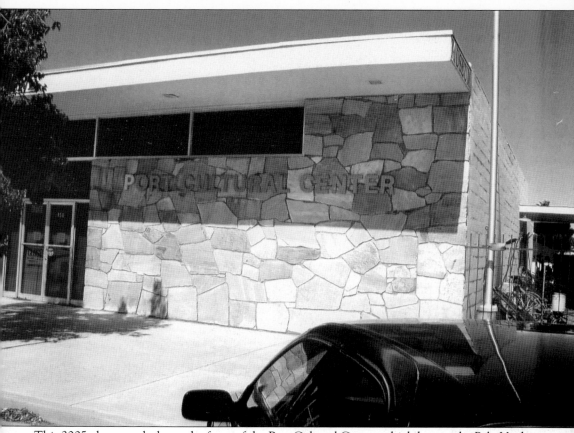

This 2005 photograph shows the front of the Port Cultural Center, which houses the Palo Verde Historical Museum and Society.

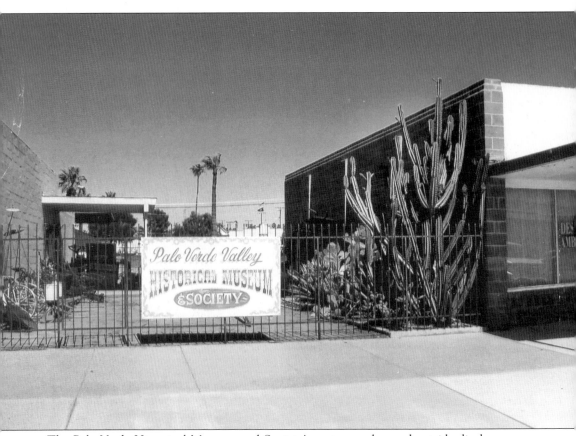

The Palo Verde Historical Museum and Society's cactus garden and outside display area are pictured here in 2005.